Editorial Project Manager
Heather Douglas

Editor in Chief
Karen J. Goldfluss, M.S. Ed.

Creative Director
Sarah M. Fournier

Illustrator
Clint McKnight

Cover Artist
Diem Pascarella

Art Coordinator
Renée Mc Elwee

Imaging
Amanda R. Harter

Publisher
Mary D. Smith, M.S. Ed.

STEPPING INTO STEM

A guided-to-independent approach to STEM-based learning

- Includes hands-on science units that introduce students to the processes of inquiry, investigation, interaction, and invention

- Encourages collaboration, journaling, and discussion

- Incorporates guided unit investigations that lead to independent team challenges

- Correlated to CCSS and NGSS

Teacher Created Resources

TCR 3980

M000110863

Author
Robert Smith

CORRELATED TO CCSS & NGSS

For correlations to the Common Core State Standards, see page 159 of this book or visit *http://www.teachercreated.com/standards/*. For correlations to the Next Generation Science Standards, see page 160 of this book.

Teacher Created Resources
12621 Western Avenue
Garden Grove, CA 92841
www.teachercreated.com
ISBN: 978-1-4206-3980-3
©2016 Teacher Created Resources
Made in U.S.A.

Teacher Created Resources

CONTENTS

Introduction

PROJECT-BASED LEARNING

As educators, we are being required to place more emphasis on science, technology, engineering, and math (STEM) in order to ensure that today's students will be prepared for their future careers. Additionally, it is important that children learn and practice the 21st-century skills of collaboration, critical thinking, problem solving, and digital literacy in their daily curricula. These collaborative skills are imperative for students to learn, but they are not without challenges. *Stepping into STEM* provides students with needed practice in these areas.

Project-based learning, simply put, is learning by doing. Project-based learning, or PBL, tends to be deeper learning that is more relevant to students, and thus remembered longer. We need to educate students to be global competitors, and to do so, we must help them to think creatively, to take risks, and to put what they are learning into practice. After all, it doesn't do much good to know a formula if you don't know when to use it. Students also need to learn the value of failure as a learning experience. Some of the ideas and efforts they make during an activity will not work. This can turn into a very positive experience since knowing what won't work, and why, may lead to the discovery of what will work!

Reading informational material provides needed background, but *doing* makes the difference. Concepts, ideas, and experiences of hands-on activities remain lodged in the brain for retrieval when needed.

In STEM curriculum, project-based learning is a must! Its collaborative style guarantees that 21st-century skills are fully integrated into the curriculum while supporting students' academic and socio-emotional growth. Furthermore, PBL allows teachers to assess what students comprehend immediately and to adapt curriculum accordingly.

CONNECTING SCIENCE, TECHNOLOGY, ENGINEERING, AND MATH

STEM activities blend four essential and related learning experiences into one activity. Technology—both simple and high-tech—provides the framework for recording information. Phones, tablets, and computers are effective in recording and comparing results. The math element might involve sequencing, patterns, or recognizing shapes, size, and volume. Comparisons are expressed in decimals, fractions, ratios, and percentages, as well as measurements, graphs, charts, and other visual representations.

THE NEED FOR INTERACTION AND COLLABORATION

Today's scientists and engineers share ideas, experiments, and solutions, as well as failures, with colleagues around the globe. Student scientists and engineers, like their professional counterparts, need experience working with partners in a collaborative and supportive environment. They need to exchange ideas, test theories, perform experiments, modify their experiments, try novel approaches—even those that may not appear useful or serious—and cooperate with each other in all aspects of the project as they seek to accomplish their objective. Depending upon the activity, students may use the *Design Process* to accomplish their objective.

A basic requirement of these collaborative efforts is a willingness to seriously consider all suggestions from the members of the team. Ideas should be considered, tried, tested, and compared for use in the project. Students should work together to select the most efficient and practical ideas, then methodically test each one for its useful application in the activity.

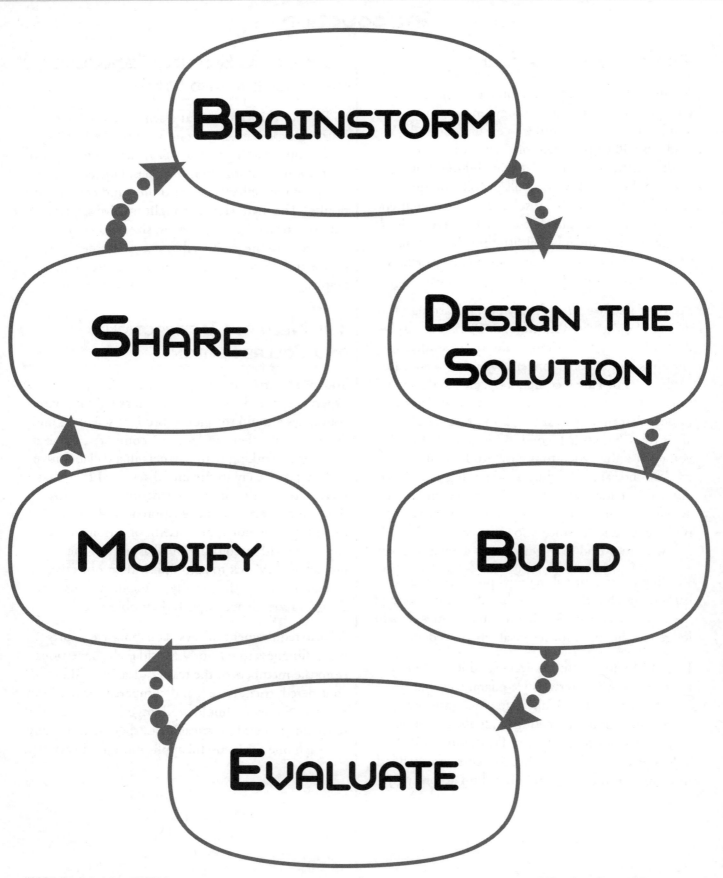

THE DESIGN PROCESS WORKSHEET

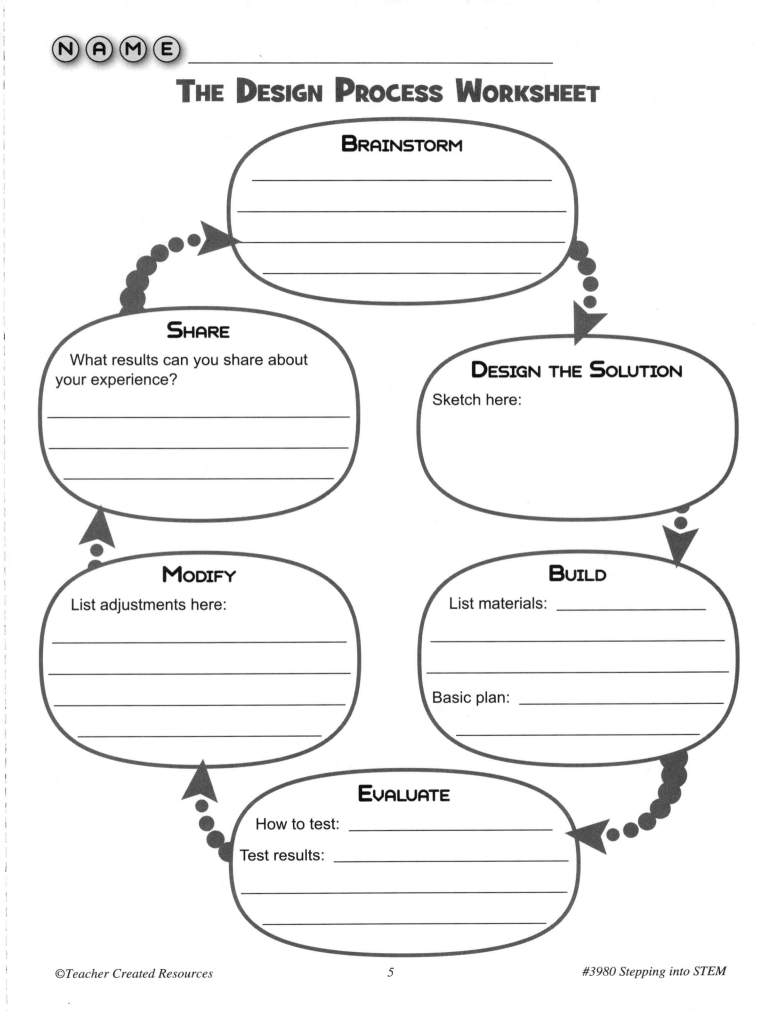

BRAINSTORM

_____
_____
_____
_____

SHARE

What results can you share about your experience?

_____
_____
_____

DESIGN THE SOLUTION

Sketch here:

MODIFY

List adjustments here:

_____
_____
_____

BUILD

List materials: _____
_____
_____

Basic plan: _____
_____

EVALUATE

How to test: _____

Test results: _____
_____
_____

GROWING CRITICAL THINKERS

While all members of a team need to be respected and heard, members of the team also need to critically examine each idea to see if the idea is feasible. This is part of the design process used by engineers and the scientific method employed by scientists.

Students need to apply their learned experiences in these activities, and serious attention should be given to testing each idea for feasibility and practicality. Students can develop this skill by considering each serious suggestion, testing it for workability, and then determining its value. Students need to examine the available materials, work with them in an organized way, record their results, and compare these results.

Critical thinkers are organized and methodical in their testing and experimentation. They examine the ideas generated in the free flow of comments and discussions. They determine which ideas can be tested and then carefully compared for useful application to the problem they are trying to solve. They keep an open mind. Critical thinkers base their judgments on observations and proven outcomes. Critical thinkers aren't negative, but they are skeptical until they observe the results of an activity.

"Show me."   "Let's check it out."

"How can we test it to see if it works?"

One of the hallmarks of a scientist is to ask questions. Another is the effort to seek answers through effective investigations, tests, and experiments. You want to encourage your student scientists to practice critical thinking by asking thoughtful questions using academic vocabulary, and by developing creative ways to test possible solutions.

THE 4 *Is*: INQUIRE • INVESTIGATE • INTERACT • INVENT

The four basic elements of an effective science or STEM activity can be categorized as Inquiry, Investigation, Interaction, and Invention.

1. INQUIRY is the process of determining what you wish to learn about a scientific or natural phenomenon. It can be as simple as watching a student's swing move back and forth, observing a schoolyard game of marbles, or sucking on a straw. Some of the same principles of science may apply to a helicopter rescue of a swimmer, a batted ball in a major-league game, or the process of getting water out of a ditch. The questions are always the same:

"Why did it happen? Will it happen every time? What happens if … you change the length of the swing, the size of the marble, the diameter of the straw, the weight of the swimmer, the diameter of the ball, or the length of the siphon hose in the ditch?"

In the simplest form, **Inquire** is a question: Why . . . ?, What if . . . ?, How . . . ?

2. INVESTIGATION is the action a scientist takes to learn more about the question. It involves the process a student scientist needs to follow. The investigation can involve background research, the process of doing an experiment, and the interpretation of the results. Reading a science text about the workings of the pendulum is not the same as actually constructing a working pendulum, adjusting it to different lengths and weights, and carefully observing its features and behavior in varying circumstances. Measuring these things in mathematical terms provides the opportunity for valid comparisons as well.

3. INTERACTION requires student scientists to collaborate with one or more classmates. Together they assess the problem or question, determine and carry out the investigation, and analyze the results.

From a practical point of view, experiments done with students are more effective with teams of two. In larger groups, one or more team members often feel left out, don't get to actually do the hands-on construction, and can end up in distracting behaviors. Teams of two require the active involvement of both individuals in all phases of the activity, all the time. An off-task student in a team can be refocused by a partner or the teacher.

It is important to have enough materials and equipment for the basic activity for each team. The materials used in the activities in this book are inexpensive and easily available to facilitate two-person teams.

4. INVENTION is the final stage of the 4 "Is" in which the science activity involves the effort to create or invent a solution, modification, or improvement. This can be the most challenging aspect of the activity. At first, suggestions tend to be far out, impractical, silly, or impossible to do with the available materials. The most effective teams discuss possible solutions and then start manipulating the materials as a form of "thinking with their hands."

The invention aspect of the activity is nearly always the final step of the activity. For instance, after multiple sessions manipulating and measuring results with a pendulum, students should have enough background and hands-on experience to invent an application for this tool. It may be a toy swing for a doll, a time-keeping mechanism for a class activity (such as a timed math exercise), or an attempt to make a perpetual-motion machine (or one that just lasts longer than anybody else's).

1 Inquire

2 Investigate

3 Interact

4 Invent

THE NEED FOR JOURNALING

Scientists keep records. They are meticulous in recording the results of their investigations and often refer back to investigations done in previous months and years. They use this information as needed for further investigations, related experiments, and in publishing their work.

Ideally, all science students should keep journals recording the investigations they have been working on. With continued practice, students will develop the habit of journaling after each period of investigation. It is easier for students to keep information in one place and to refer back to previous investigations for discussion purposes and records. Consider having students use 3-ring binders to keep unit pages together with additional notes, ideas, and sketches.

It is suggested that a separate entry be made for each investigation session. Have students enter the date and investigation title for each new entry. Include a key question for each activity. This is the starting point for each investigation. As students proceed, they should record, using adequate details, the process and materials used to investigate the question. Encourage students to use appropriate vocabulary when journaling.

The variations in technique, the engineering adjustments, the technology employed, and the results of each modification should be recorded. The mathematical applications should also be noted. If the length of the pendulum fishing line was doubled or cut in half, this is critical information. If the weight was doubled from 8 grams to 16 grams, this should be noted, and the effect on the pendulum's swing distance and duration should be recorded. The results of each trial should be briefly recorded.

The most important information in the journal should be the conclusions of the research team about the answer to the testable questions the team was investigating. Individual researchers may draw separate conclusions about these questions, but the conclusions need to be based on objective facts and recorded information.

THE DESIGN PROCESS REVIEW

The journal entries should be the "notes" student scientists use when sharing their information during the class discussion which is called the *Design Process Review*. The teacher can act as the moderator of this discussion and should ensure that each student gets an opportunity to share his or her experiences, results, and scientific observations. This discussion works well as a 10-minute closure activity at the end of each period.

Encourage all students to take turns sharing the results of their activities and the conclusions they drew from their experiments. Data summaries may include photos, videos, or other relevant materials.

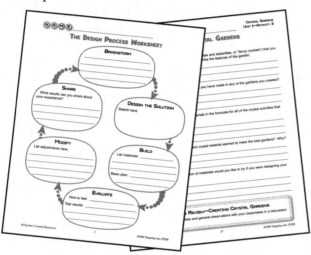

Model and encourage serious reporting. Encourage students to incorporate new vocabulary into their discussions, their journaling, and their presentation pieces.

The writing (journaling) and the review are vital elements in the design process. They provide students with the opportunity to share their experiences, and these activities serve as an excellent part of the assessment process. It is suggested that you allow at least 15 to 20 minutes to complete these activities.

You may choose to act as moderator. You can allow students to share as teams or as individuals about each activity and other activities they have done on related subjects. You may also use smaller groups with student moderators.

KEEPING THINGS IN PERSPECTIVE!

A STEM class will rarely be perfectly quiet! In fact, the low buzz of purposeful conversation is an indicator that students are actively engaged. The teacher serves as the facilitator, providing guidance, crucial information, and directions at the outset. It is important to regularly check on each group to offer encouragement, advice, correction, and support.

Teachers need to evaluate how students are doing as teams proceed with investigations. In addition to guiding the learning process, it is also very important to draw closure on the activity by moderating the final portion of the *Design Process Review* in which you draw conclusions and highlight the core learning concepts embedded in the activity.

Unsuccessful periods happen in any class, no matter how capable the instructor or how gifted the students. Things can go wrong, bells ring forever, announcements from the intercom break the flow of instruction and construction, and all the other distractions of school life can occur. You may get a true scientific discussion going but have it go off into areas unrelated to the thrust of the investigation.

But there are also those times when you encounter the pleasant experience of no one paying any attention to the distraction. A visitor or principal enters the room, observes the activity for a moment, and either leaves or joins a group. The science discussion reverts to the main idea and goes smoothly or vigorously along, driven by students who are focused and on task. Yes, it happens!

Students can really "get into" science. They enjoy the openness involved in the activity, the collegial nature of working on a project, the materials they get to manipulate, and the mental stimulation of solving a problem or creating a better product. A good, productive, stimulating science period can make their day—and yours, too.

How to Use This Book

Stepping into STEM is arranged with flexibility in mind. One method is to move from lesson to lesson in each unit and proceed through the units in order. However, the number and order of units completed throughout the year is completely dependent on classroom and curriculum needs. You may want to choose the activities with which you are more familiar or those that better fit your school schedule. The organization of each unit moves from teacher-directed activities to more student-driven activities to a final challenge activity that allows students to create their own unique product or invention. Students should be encouraged to follow the Design Process while doing the activities in each unit.

PACING UNITS AND LESSONS

Planning the length of time for completion of each unit can be flexible. You may choose some or all of the units and pace them througout the year, building each unit into your science curriculum. If a unit topic fits in well with what is currently being taught, embed it into the schedule where possible. Since these unit investigations were developed to foster a STEM approach to learning, they do not have to be tied to any specific time frame or subject in the science curriculum.

To get the most out of a unit, it is suggested that a few sessions be allotted to complete the activities. These can be spread out as needed. Usually, an activity can be done in about an hour. For those fortunate enough to have a one-and-a-half-hour period, students will have more time to explore the variations in each project and to extend their creative explorations. Remember that the unit activities can be broken into more than one session! Be sure to allow serious time for journaling and recording information in each period.

VOCABULARY AND DISCUSSIONS

Share and discuss the STEM Vocabulary List (page 15) and unit vocabulary lists with students. Identify and use the terms frequently throughout the sessions to reinforce essential subject-area vocabulary. Enlarge each unit list to create posters for student reference, or photocopy a list for each student to keep in his or her journaling notebook.

Encourage discussions within groups and between groups if the discussions are focused on the topic. At the end of each activity, allow time for the teacher-moderated review activities, in which individuals share their experiments, designs, results, and conclusions based on their research.

A general activity period could allow 5 to 7 minutes for teacher introduction and review of previous learning, 5 minutes to efficiently distribute supplies, and 30 to 40 minutes to complete the activity involving science, technology, engineering, and math. The remaining time should be devoted to science journaling.

TEACHER AND STUDENT RUBRICS

Use the teacher rubric on page 16 to evaluate team progress, time-on-task, and student interaction, and to reinforce STEM objectives. Students who are focused on the objective and are methodically trying different ways to solve a problem are doing science. So are those who are responding a bit randomly to their own ideas and trying them out.

As student groups work through each investigation, they should complete the student rubric on page 17 to reinforce the processes they used and to reflect on the procedures they followed.

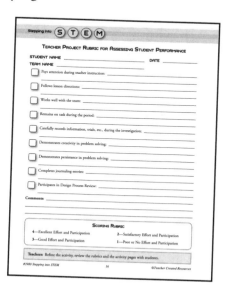

NOTE: Explain both rubrics to students before starting the units. It is important for them to know how their work will be evaluated and what steps they should follow as they work on a unit investigation.

CHALLENGE ACTIVITY

Each of the units culminates in a challenge assignment. Students are asked to create a new version of a product or extend experimentation based on the activities in the unit. Students are advised to look over their journals and other documentation collected during the unit and pick an extension to do. There are also some directions/suggestions in each challenge lesson to guide students who need them.

Allow time for imagination, frustration, and so forth during the building and testing periods of the challenge assignments. Use the grading rubric for creativity, success, effort, and on-task work time.

TEAM MANAGEMENT AND MATERIALS

In this explosive era of scientific knowledge and discovery, teamwork matters, all children need the kinesthetic experiences and collaborative interaction with their peers that are essential aspects of science instruction.

The activities in this series were designed to maximize student participation. Students will work in pairs or small collaborative teams. The collaborative process is essential to construct the apparatus and create the models. Four hands and two minds working together are more efficient and effective than individuals proceeding alone.

Materials used for the STEM activities in this book are not from expensive science kits. Those kits tend to not provide enough materials to engage all students simultaneously. Virtually all of the materials used in this series are available at relatively inexpensive cost at local big-box and discount stores. Other materials are available in local hardware or craft stores.

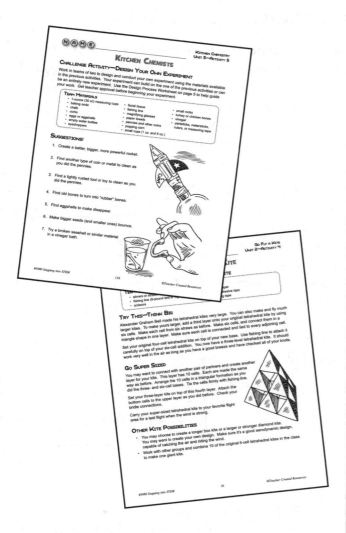

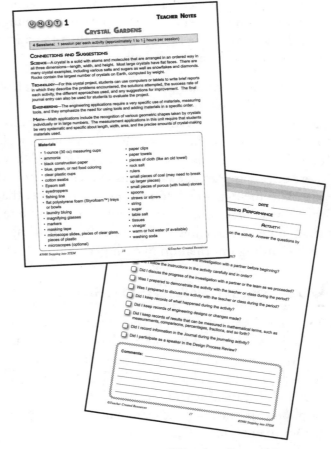

Lesson Notes for the Teacher

LESSON 1—GUIDED ACTIVITY

The first lesson is designed so that the teacher can guide and control the pace of the activity and ensure that students know how to function in this type of science activity and with these materials. It is more teacher-directed in terms of time and following specific directions than later lessons in the unit.

Providing guidance through the beginning phases of each unit will set the stage for student groups to continue with their investigations and discussions throughout the units. This is also an opportunity for the teacher to note which teams or students might be struggling and to provide more assistance to them.

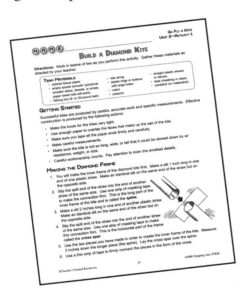

LESSONS—YOUR TURN

Review students' findings and ideas related to their investigations in Activity 1. Discuss how students will be exploring how a project works under various conditions. This can be an independent collaborative group activity. Students work in pairs.

The next two or three lessons allow students to work at their own pace as they do the activities. The teacher circulates through the room giving advice, encouragement, and correction as needed. Students work in pairs.

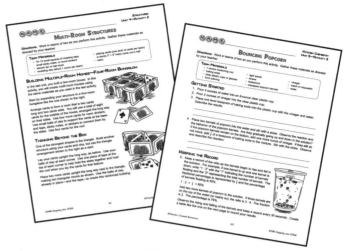

FINAL LESSON—THE CHALLENGE

The final lesson in each unit involves a Challenge Activity in which students apply what they have learned in earlier lessons to solve a specific problem or make the fastest, best, or most unique application of the concepts learned. Students should work in pairs.

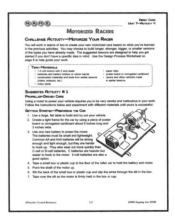

ABOUT TEAMS

Although there are always students who prefer to work alone— and have difficulty working with others—most students quickly find that these projects need 3 or 4 hands working in unison to work well. Most students also realize that the opportunity to share ideas and experiences helps their own performance and is reflected in their success in a project.

You may want to have students switch partners when you start a new unit, or after partners have been together for a few units.

Whenever possible, keep the teams small (two people) and therefore able to keep their hands and minds occupied and on task.

ABOUT TEAMS *(cont.)*

The activities in this series are designed for full participation by all students with all students actively engaged at all times. All students will use the materials and should have access to the necessary equipment. Students work in collaborative teams in order to facilitate learning, but all students are actively engaged with all aspects of the projects.

There are very few lone scientists working in private anymore in this age of scientific and technological discovery. Teamwork matters—and all children need the kinesthetic experiences and collaborative interaction with their peers that are essential aspects of science instruction.

ELL TIPS

Review vocabulary with ELL (English Language Learner) students to assure understanding. Ask ELL students to describe the intent and focus of the project. Pair ELL students with EO (English Only) students where needed. Strongly encourage the journaling aspect of the activities and the Design Process Reviews.

A NOTE ABOUT MATERIALS

Many materials used in these projects are easy to find and, in most cases, are reusable. Some are school supplies. There should be a sufficient supply for each team. Virtually all of the materials used in this series are available at relatively inexpensive cost in local stores—especially wholesale places and some dollar discount stores. A few are available in local hardware stores.

See individual units for a listing of specific materials. Be sure to collect all materials ahead of time, and consider ways to distribute, use, and store materials prior to introducing each new unit. If possible, establish an area in the classroom where materials can be accessed easily.

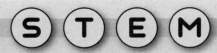
Addressing Standards

NEXT GENERATION SCIENCE STANDARDS

The National Research Council of the National Academy of Sciences published "A Framework for K–12 Science Education: Practices, Crosscutting Concepts, and Core Ideas." (NRC, 2012)

Its purpose was to serve as a guide for the 26 states presently collaborating to develop the Next Generation Science Standards. The framework defined science "to mean the traditional natural sciences: physics, chemistry, biology, and (more recently) earth, space, and environmental sciences."

The council used the term *engineering* to mean "any engagement in a systematic practice of design to achieve solutions to particular human problems."

They used the term *technology* "to include all types of human-made systems and processes—not simply modern computational and communications devices. Technologies result when engineers apply their understanding of the natural world and of human behavior to design ways to satisfy human needs and wants."

One of the critical elements of the Next Generation Science Standards is the effort to develop science practices in students. These are the behaviors that scientists actually engage in as they do their investigations. When students or scientists engage in science, they are deeply involved in inquiry as they use a range of skills and knowledge at the same time.

The engineering practices "are the behaviors that engineers engage in as they apply science and math to design solutions to problems." Engineering design has similarities to scientific inquiry. However, there are differences in the two subjects. Scientific inquiry involves creating a question that can be solved through investigation such as, "What happens to an eggshell when you put it in vinegar?" Try to ask "what" questions instead of "why" questions. They are open-ended and focus on what can be observed during experimentation.

Engineering design involves creating a question that can be solved through design.

"How can I make a structure that can withstand a strong earthquake?"

"What happens when I make my structure by constructing it in a different shape than a square?"

These are engineering questions although they may produce scientific information. Strengthening the engineering component in these standards helps students recognize the interrelationship between the four cornerstones of STEM instruction: Science, Technology, Engineering, and Math.

The **Disciplinary Core Ideas (DCI)** in the Next Generation Science Standards are broad essential ideas in science instruction across several grade levels and areas of science instruction including the life sciences, earth and space science, the physical sciences, engineering, and technology.

Cross-cutting Concepts are ideas that bridge the boundaries between science and engineering, and help students connect different ideas in the sciences into a recognizable pattern. They provide students with an organizational framework for connecting science and engineering concepts into coherent patterns.

The 7 Cross-cutting Concepts

1. Patterns
2. Cause and Effect
3. Scale, Proportion, and Quantity
4. Systems and System Models
5. Energy and Matter
6. Structure and Function
7. Stability and Change

Most good science activities exhibit examples of several of these concepts, of course, and students should begin to notice these concepts as they do the experiments in this book. Their journals should specify one or more of these concepts as they write about a project.

Addressing Standards

COMMON CORE STATE STANDARDS

The math applications in doing complete, detailed science activities is as essential as the apparatus and materials used in the activities. The emphasis on math and reading literacy is built into the Common Core as a prominent aspect of the near-national consensus that Common Core provides. The application of both skills is essential to STEM teaching.

Teachers may find that they need to explain the application of a wide variety of math concepts as they come up in STEM activities. These math activities may involve measurement, computing percentages, working with fractions and mixed numbers, measuring and converting units of time, measuring and comparing distances, working with metric units, and many other math concepts. Students often know the processes in these math activities but have no idea how to use them in real-life or science applications.

The Common Core State Standards have placed a strong emphasis on math *applications*, not just the mechanics of a skill. Utilizing math in comparing various results in a science activity will increase understanding of many concepts. Metric measurement—the common system used in science—becomes second nature to students who routinely use it to measure and compare distance, volume, and capacity, for example. Percentages, ratios, and other comparative measurements have more meaning when applied to hands-on activities.

The Common Core Standards are likewise focused on informational reading in science (as well as social studies). Students need to become familiar with sources beyond the textbook to research science information. These involve both paper and digital sources.

The writing standards of the Common Core also expect students to routinely write effectively on science topics. The activities in this book provide a guided opportunity to take notes and write brief reports on each activity while including all relevant details.

Common Core State Standards emphasize the development of speaking and listening skills, and encourage discussion and collaboration. *Stepping into STEM* provides opportunities for students to share their collective writings with each other in colloquium discussions.

STANDARDS CORRELATIONS

Correlations for both the Common Core State Standards and the Next Generation Science Standards are provided for the units in this book.

General standards correlations for each unit can be found on pages 159–160. You can also visit *www.teachercreated.com/standards* for more comprehensive Common Core State Standards correlations charts.

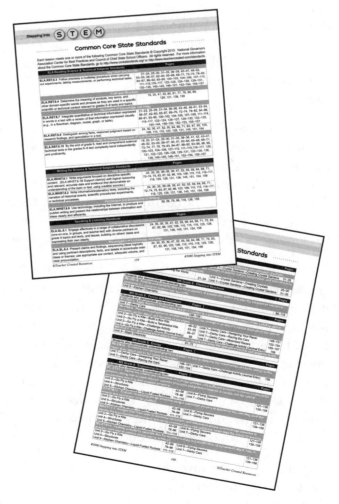

STEM Vocabulary

The following vocabulary words are used in STEM explorations. Discuss these terms and use them often during the activities and in your journals.

<u>brainstorm</u>—a method of problem solving in which all members of a group spontaneously discuss ideas

<u>collaborate</u>—to work with one or more members in a team to assess the problem or question, determine the nature of the investigation, and analyze results

<u>communicate</u>—to talk with others

<u>design</u>—an outline or plan

<u>design process</u>—a series of steps used by engineers to create products and/or processes

<u>efficient</u>—working well without unusual effort

<u>evaluate</u>—to make a judgment

<u>hypothesis</u>—a temporary prediction that can be tested; a serious scientific guess or idea that works as a starting point for further investigation

<u>innovation</u>—an improvement of an existing product, system, or way of doing something

<u>inquiry</u>—the process of determining what you wish to learn about a scientific or natural phenomenon

<u>invent</u>—the effort to design a solution, modification, or improvement

<u>investigate</u>—the action a scientist takes to learn more about the question

<u>manipulate</u>—to control or change something, often with the hands

<u>modify</u>—to change or adjust

<u>observation</u>—scientific information gathered during an experiment

<u>reaction</u>—a chemical change

<u>scientific method</u>—a series of steps used by scientists to carry out experiments

<u>unique</u>—special or different; unusual; one of a kind

<u>variable</u>—something that can be changed

TEACHER RUBRIC FOR ASSESSING STUDENT PERFORMANCE

STUDENT NAME _____ DATE _____

TEAM NAME _____

☐ Pays attention during teacher instruction: _____
_____

☐ Follows lesson directions: _____
_____

☐ Works well with the team: _____
_____

☐ Remains on task during the period: _____
_____

☐ Carefully records information, trials, etc., during the investigation: _____
_____

☐ Demonstrates creativity in problem solving: _____
_____

☐ Demonstrates persistence in problem solving: _____
_____

☐ Completes journaling entries: _____
_____

☐ Participates in Design Process Review: _____
_____

Comments: _____
_____
_____

SCORING RUBRIC

4—Excellent Effort and Participation   **2**—Satisfactory Effort and Participation

3—Good Effort and Participation   **1**—Poor or No Effort and Participation

Teachers: Before the activity, review the rubrics and the activity pages with students.

NAME _____   **DATE** _____

STUDENT RUBRIC FOR ASSESSING PERFORMANCE

UNIT:	ACTIVITY:

Directions: Use this rubric to guide you as you work on the activity. Answer the questions by placing an "X" in each box as you go along.

- ☐ Did I read the project instructions carefully?
- ☐ Did I discuss the instructions with a partner or team?
- ☐ Did I set up the materials for the investigation with a partner before beginning?
- ☐ Did I follow the instructions in the activity carefully and in order?
- ☐ Did I discuss the progress of the investigation with a partner or the team as we proceeded?
- ☐ Was I prepared to demonstrate the activity with the teacher or class during the period?
- ☐ Was I prepared to discuss the activity with the teacher or class during the period?
- ☐ Did I keep records of what happened during the activity?
- ☐ Did I keep records of engineering designs or changes made?
- ☐ Did I keep records of results that can be measured in mathematical terms, such as measurements, comparisons, percentages, fractions, and so forth?
- ☐ Did I record information in the Journal during the journaling activity?
- ☐ Did I participate as a speaker in the Design Process Review?

Comments: _____

_____

_____

_____

_____

 **1**

CRYSTAL GARDENS

4 Sessions: 1 session per each activity (approximately 1 to $1\frac{1}{2}$ hours per session)

CONNECTIONS AND SUGGESTIONS

SCIENCE—A crystal is a solid with atoms and molecules that are arranged in an ordered way in all three dimensions—length, width, and height. Most large crystals have flat faces. There are many crystal examples, including various salts and sugars as well as snowflakes and diamonds. Rocks contain the largest number of crystals on Earth, computed by weight.

TECHNOLOGY—For this crystal project, students can use computers or tablets to write brief reports in which they describe the problems encountered, the solutions attempted, the success rate of each activity, the different approaches used, and any suggestions for improvement. The final journal entry can also be used for students to evaluate the project.

ENGINEERING—The engineering applications require a very specific use of materials, measuring tools, and they emphasize the need for using tools and adding materials in a specific order.

MATH—Math applications include the recognition of various geometric shapes taken by crystals individually or in large numbers. The measurement applications in this unit require that students be very systematic and specific about length, width, area, and the precise amounts of crystal-making materials used.

Materials

- 1-ounce (30 cc) measuring cups
- ammonia
- black construction paper
- blue, green, or red food coloring
- clear plastic cups
- cotton swabs
- Epsom salt
- eyedroppers
- fishing line
- flat polystyrene foam (Styrofoam™) trays or bowls
- laundry bluing
- magnifying glasses
- markers
- masking tape
- microscope slides, pieces of clear glass, pieces of plastic
- microscopes (optional)

- paper clips
- paper towels
- pieces of cloth (like an old towel)
- rock salt
- rulers
- small pieces of coal (may need to break up larger pieces)
- small pieces of porous (with holes) stones
- spoons
- straws or stirrers
- string
- sugar
- table salt
- tissues
- vinegar
- warm or hot water (if available)
- washing soda

• • • • • UNIT 1 VOCABULARY • • • • •

compounds—chemical combinations of two or more elements

crystals—solids formed from molecules or atoms arranged in a regular, repeating, three-dimensional pattern

diffusion—the spreading out of molecules within a solution

durable—long-lasting

horizontal—flat, even with the earth

hypothesis—a serious scientific guess or idea

reaction—a chemical change

reinforce—to support or strengthen

stalactites— icicle-shaped formations that grow down from the ceiling of caves (usually limestone), hot springs, and some man-made structures

stalagmites—icicle-shaped formations that grow up from the floor of caves (usually limestone), hot springs, and some man-made structures

vertical—straight up-and-down

DISCUSSION PROMPT:

Crystals can be found all over the world, and people use them for everything from jewelry to computer chips. In the past, some of the most expensive crystals (like diamonds) had to be mined. Nowadays, scientists are able to produce synthetic (artificial) diamonds— also known as cultured diamonds, cultivated diamonds, or diamond simulants. This is done through a process involving high pressure and high temperature. Even though these synthetics often have fewer impurities and are less expensive than authentic crystals, many people still only want authentic diamonds (or other crystals and gems). Why do you think this is so? Also, why do you think the diamond industry doesn't like synthetic diamonds?

CRYSTALS

Crystals are materials whose atoms or molecules are arranged in a highly ordered structure. They can be identified by their geometric shape; they have flat faces with sharp angles. Although all crystals have those characteristics, they can look very different from each other. Examples of crystals are snowflakes, diamonds, and table salt.

Most crystals are found in Earth's bedrock. The majority of igneous rocks are formed from magma, and the degree of crystallization depends on the conditions in which they solidified. Metamorphic rocks come from existing rocks and are the result of a transformation from the pressure and heat beneath the surface of Earth. When they form, rocks that contain certain minerals can recrystallize. For example, limestone can form crystals in marble, and sandstone (which is made of sand and quartz) can form quartzite. Limestone and sandstone are examples of sedimentary rocks, which form from sediment on Earth's surface or in bodies of water.

Some rock crystals form from the precipitation of fluids—often when these fluids evaporate. Other crystals form in the shape of snowflakes (a single crystal) and ice cubes (a polycrystal).

Almost any solid material can crystalize. At one point, it was thought that the center of Earth was a single, 1,500-mile-wide iron crystal. Studies now show that it is not a single solid but perhaps is made up of smaller crystals.

Crystals often have beautiful, vivid colors, especially a group of crystals called gemstones. Common gemstones are rubies (which are often red), emeralds (which are often green), and sapphires (which are often blue). Diamonds are gemstones, too. They are often clear, but they can also come in yellow, brown, and pink hues.

Use a computer or tablet to search for information on the Internet to help you as you complete the activities in this unit. Helpful search items include:

amorphous	crystalline	polycrystalline	stalagmites
crystals	diamonds	snowflakes	sugar
crystal structure	Epsom salt	stalactites	table salt

 _____

EXPLORING THE WORLD OF CRYSTALS

Directions: Work in teams of two as you perform these activities. Gather these materials as directed by your teacher.

> **TEAM MATERIALS**
> - black construction paper
> - blue, green, or red food coloring
> - clear plastic cups (1- or 2-oz. work well)
> - Epsom salt
> - eyedroppers
> - glass or plastic microscope slides
>
> - magnifying glasses
> - microscopes (if available)
> - paper towels
> - pieces of clear plastic
> - rock salt
> - straws or stirrers
>
> - sugar
> - table salt
> - water (warm or hot works best)

CAUTION: When handling the chemical compounds, keep hands away from the face and eyes. Wash your hands when done.

Time Note: The *first* activity works well on a hot, sunny day. It can also be done with a warm stove or heater (if available) in wintertime. This activity can be started on one day and completed on the next day. The *second* activity works well over a long weekend. The solution can be made on the first day, then examined along the way or after a few days. Make sure your name is on your solution so you can easily find it among the other solutions.

GETTING STARTED

Place a pinch of table salt on a microscope slide, a piece of black construction paper, or a small piece of clear plastic. Use a magnifying glass (or microscope) to examine the salt. Look for shapes and regular features common to each individual salt crystal. Look at several individual salt crystals. Look for features that are common to all or most of the crystals.

Which geometric shape do most salt crystals have? _____

Sketch a few of the salt crystals.

What similarities do the salt crystals have?

_____

_____

_____

What differences do they have?

_____

_____

_____

_____

 NAME _____

EXPLORING THE WORLD OF CRYSTALS

ANOTHER TYPE OF SALT CRYSTAL

Place a pinch or two of Epsom salt on another piece of black construction paper. Examine these crystals with the magnifying glass. Sketch these salt crystals. Which geometric shape do most Epsom salt crystals have?

_____

Compare them to the table salt.

How are they similar? _____

How are they different? _____

SWEET CRYSTALS

Place a pinch of sugar crystals on a third piece of black construction paper. Examine these crystals with the magnifying glass. Sketch these sugar crystals.

Which geometric shape do most sugar crystals have?

_____

Compare them to the table salt and Epsom salt.

How are they similar? _____

How are they different? _____

ROCK SALT

Place a spoonful of rock salt on a piece of black construction paper. Examine these crystals with the magnifying glass. Sketch these salt crystals.

Which geometric shape do most of the rock salt crystals have?

_____

Compare them to the table salt, Epsom salt, and sugar crystals.

How are they similar? _____

How are they different? _____

EXPLORING THE WORLD OF CRYSTALS

EPSOM SALT CRYSTALS

1. Place a pinch of Epsom salt and a half-dropper full of water into a one-ounce clear cup. Warm or hot water works best, if available.

2. Stir the Epsom salt and the water until the salt is completely dissolved. You can use an eyedropper, straw, stirrer, or toothpick to stir the solution.

3. Use the eyedropper to remove some of the solution and place it on a microscope slide, on a piece of glass or plastic, or in the bottom of a clear plastic cup. Put the slide, glass, or plastic in a warm place—in direct sunlight, if possible.

4. Let the solution dry; this may take some time and have to be continued on another day.

5. When the liquid is dry, examine the crystals on the slide, glass, or plastic. In the box below, sketch what you see.

6. Describe the crystals in detail for color, shapes, formations, and feel.

_____

_____

_____

_____

_____

 NAME _____

EXPLORING THE WORLD OF CRYSTALS

JOURNAL ENTRY

1. Which of the crystals did you find the most interesting in this unit? Why?

   _____

   _____

   _____

   _____

2. What other crystal shapes or crystal colors have you seen at home, at school, or in a piece of jewelry?

   _____

   _____

   _____

3. What do all the crystals seem to have in common? How are they similar?

   _____

   _____

   _____

   _____

4. How do crystals vary? Use examples. Think size, color, hardness, and any other features.

   _____

   _____

   _____

   _____

DESIGN PROCESS REVIEW—EXPLORING THE WORLD OF CRYSTALS

Share your journal entries and general observations with your classmates in a discussion led by your teacher.

CREATING CRYSTALS

MAKING A SALT GARDEN

Directions: Work in teams of two as you perform these activities. Gather these materials as directed by your teacher.

TEAM MATERIALS

- blue, green, or red food coloring
- clear plastic cups (1- or 2-oz. work well)
- eyedroppers
- magnifying glasses
- polystyrene foam (Styrofoam™) trays
- small pieces of coal

- small pieces of porous (with holes) stones, such as pumice or brick
- spoons
- table salt
- tissues

- vinegar
- water (warm or hot preferred)

1. Fill a plastic cup half full of water, preferably warm or hot water.

2. Use a spoon to put two spoonfuls of regular table salt into the water. Stir the salt until it is thoroughly mixed into the solution. Keep adding salt a little bit at a time until no more can be dissolved.

3. Add two eyedroppers worth of vinegar to the solution. (Each dropper will actually hold half a dropper of vinegar because air takes up some of the space. Just fill the dropper twice.) Note: The vinegar serves to clear any oil off the coal or stones so that the water can move freely through the stones.

4. Place two small pieces of coal, or two soft rocks, and two wads of tissue on a flat, foam tray. Pour the solution over each of the objects.

5. Leave the trays in a warm place to dry for a few days. Observe the results as the solution dries. Use the box below to draw sketches of what you observe as the solution is drying.

★ ★ ★ YOU WILL USE THESE MATERIALS IN THE NEXT ACTIVITY. ★ ★ ★

CREATING CRYSTALS

SALT GARDEN CRYSTAL FORMATION

Examine your crystal solution that you poured on the coal, rocks, and wads of tissue. Use a magnifying glass. Try not to disturb the crystals. Record these results for each examination.

Where have crystals started forming? How many days did it take? Describe the **shape**, **color**, and **formation** of the crystals.

First Examination (Date: _____)

_____

_____

_____

_____

_____

Count the faces of several crystals. How many faces or facets did most of the crystals have? _____

In the box above, sketch what you observed during your First Examination.

TRY THIS

Refresh your crystal garden by adding two eyedroppers full of water carefully to one corner of the container. Add 1 or 2 drops of food coloring to the water. Leave the tray in a warm place.

Let the garden sit for a day. Record what you observe on the lines below. In the box below, sketch what you observed during your Second Examination.

Second Examination (Date: _____)

_____

_____

_____

_____

_____

_____

CREATING CRYSTALS

MAKING YOUR OWN STALAGMITES AND STALACTITES

Directions: Work in teams of two as you perform these activities. Gather these materials as directed by your teacher. (For a visual demonstration of a similar experiment, you may wish to view the following video: ***https://www.youtube.com/watch?v=nYxVtYUG5bg***.)

TEAM MATERIALS

- blue, green, or red food coloring
- clear plastic cups (8- or 10-ounce)
- eyedroppers
- fishing line
- paper clips

- paper towels
- pieces of cloth (like an old towel or T-shirt)
- polystyrene foam (Styrofoam™) trays
- spoons

- straws or stirrers
- table salt
- vinegar
- washing soda
- water

Stalactites are mineral formations growing from the ceilings of some caves. Stalagmites are mineral formations that build up from the floor of these caves. These formations are the results of dripping water and mineral deposits.

You can create your own model of these formations with washing soda and water. (Washing soda is a laundry booster used to clean difficult stains.)

STEP 1

a. Twist a thin piece of soft cloth (like an old towel) into a twisted rope about 3 inches wide and 1 foot long. Cut three pieces of fishing line or string, each about 3 inches long. Tie each end of the "rope" with one piece of the fishing line or string. Tie the third piece of string or fishing line in the middle of the "rope." (You can also use a thick, good-quality paper towel for the rope. Thick yarn may work, as well.)

b. Slip a large paper clip onto each end of the rope, through the fishing line ties. Have the clip slip the long way over the end, in line with the length of the rope.

c. Fill two clear 8- or 10-ounce plastic cups with hot tap water almost to the top. Leave about an inch (2.5 cm) of space at the top.

STEP 2

a. Add 1 drop of food coloring to each cup of hot water. Use a different color in each cup. Observe the diffusion of the food coloring through the water.

b. Use a plastic spoon to place about $\frac{1}{2}$ cup (about 20 to 24 level teaspoons) of washing soda in each cup of hot water. **Stir with a straw or spoon after you add each teaspoon to make sure the washing soda is thoroughly dissolved in the water.** Add teaspoons of washing soda until no more will dissolve—up to 24 teaspoons. Do this carefully and keep track of the amount you used.

c. Feel the solution with your fingers. It should be very soapy with the washing soda dissolved in the water.

CREATING CRYSTALS

MAKING YOUR OWN STALAGMITES AND STALACTITES *(cont.)*

STEP 3

a. Place one twisted end of the cloth rope or paper towel (with the attached paper clip) in one cup. The paper clip should help the rope stay near the bottom.

b. Place the other end of cloth rope or paper towel in the second cup. Make sure both ends touch the bottoms of the cups.

c. Place a polystyrene foam tray between the two cups. There should be a slight dip or bend of the rope in the middle above the plate or bowl.

Sketch your setup in the box below.

Leave this crystal experiment undisturbed. Do not touch it. It may take a night or a weekend for the crystals to start to form. You will examine this formation during Activity 3.

CREATING CRYSTALS

GROWING FANCY CRYSTALS

Directions: Work in teams of two as you perform these activities. Gather these materials as directed by your teacher.

TEAM MATERIALS
- blue, green, or red food coloring
- clear plastic cups (8 ounce)
- cotton swabs (Q-Tips®)
- eyedroppers
- food coloring
- masking tape
- paper towels
- polystyrene foam (Styrofoam™) trays
- straws or stirrers (6 or 7 inches long)
- string
- sugar
- table salt
- water

NOTE: Like the previous activity, you will start the crystal formation today and examine the results in the next investigation.

GETTING STARTED

1. Cut a piece of string to be about 3 inches long.
2. Tie the top of the string to one end of a 6- or 7-inch straw or stirrer. Tie or tape the string about 2 inches from one end of the stirrer.
3. Use masking tape to attach a cotton swab vertically to the middle of the stirrer.
4. Tear half of a paper towel and fold it or twist it. Use masking tape to attach the paper towel to the stirrer about 2 inches from the other end. The paper towel can be taped so that half points down and half points up.
5. Attach the straw—with the string, swab, and paper towel—to the edge of the long side of a tray. Gently and carefully tape each end of the straw to the tray.

MAKING THE CRYSTALS

1. Pour 3 ounces (90 mL) of hot or very warm water into a cup.
2. Pour 1 ounce (30 cc) of sugar into the water. Use a straw to stir the solution until the sugar crystals completely dissolve in the water.

3. Add 2 drops of food coloring to the solution. Observe as the food coloring diffuses through the solution.
4. Pour the solution into the tray. Make sure the string, swab, and paper towel are touching the solution. Leave the gardens undisturbed for a day or a weekend.

CREATING CRYSTALS

JOURNAL ENTRY

1. What do you think will happen to the crystal garden? Explain your answer.

   _____

   _____

   _____

2. In the "fancy crystals" which of the three materials—string, cotton swab, or paper towel—will have crystals? Why?

   _____

   _____

   _____

3. What color and shape will the crystals be? Explain your reasoning.

   _____

   _____

   _____

4. Will the crystals be hard or soft? Why?

   _____

   _____

   _____

5. Do you think this crystal garden could be made with table salt, rock salt, or Epsom salts? Explain your answer. How could you find out?

   _____

   _____

   _____

DESIGN PROCESS REVIEW—CREATING CRYSTALS

Share your journal entries and general observations with your classmates in a discussion led by your teacher.

CREATING CRYSTAL GARDENS

Directions: Work in teams of two as you perform these activities.

SALT GARDEN CRYSTAL FORMATION—Third Examination (Date: _____)

Take a moment to examine your crystal solution that you poured on the coal, rocks, and tissue. Use a magnifying glass. Try not to disturb the crystals. Record the results.

_____

_____

_____

Where did the crystals start forming? How many days did it take? Describe the shape, color, and formation of the crystals. Count the faces on the crystals. What is the usual amount?

_____

_____

In the box to the right, sketch what you observed during your Third Examination.

STALAGMITE AND STALACTITE GARDENS—First Examination (Date: _____)

Carefully examine your crystal garden grown with washing soda. Look at the shapes of the structures formed, the colors of the structures, and the individual crystals. Use your magnifying glass.

1. What is/are the basic shape or shapes of the large formation? Describe the general look of the formation.

_____

_____

2. In the box to the right, sketch the formation.

3. Use your magnifying glass to examine individual crystals of the stalagmites and stalactites. What crystal shapes can you see? Are the crystals small or large? What color are the crystals?

_____

_____

 _____

CREATING CRYSTAL GARDENS

EXAMINING YOUR "FANCY CRYSTAL" TRAY—First Examination (Date: _____)

Use your magnifying glass to examine the crystals.

1. Which material—the string, the cotton swab, or the paper towel—has the most crystals? Why do you think it had the most crystals?

    _____

    _____

2. What color and shape are the crystals?

    _____

3. Are there crystals on the tray itself? Has all or most of the water evaporated from the tray?

    _____

4. Can you separate a single crystal from the others? What do you notice about this crystal? What geometric figure does it most resemble?

    _____

    _____

In the box below, sketch what you observed.

 _____

CREATING CRYSTAL GARDENS

CREATING A SPECTACULAR CRYSTAL GARDEN

Directions: Work in teams of two as you perform these activities. Gather these materials as directed by your teacher.

TEAM MATERIALS
- $\frac{1}{2}$ ounce of ammonia
- 1 ounce (30 cc) table salt
- 1 ounce (30 mL) of laundry bluing
- 1 ounce (30 mL) of warm water
- 6- or 8-ounce clear plastic cup
- flat Styrofoam™ tray or bowl
- food coloring (optional)
- straw or stirrer
- white facial tissues

GETTING STARTED

1. Pour the water into the 8-oz. plastic cup. Add some food coloring, if desired.

2. Pour the salt into the water and stir until all or nearly all of the salt is dissolved.

3. Pour in the ammonia. Stir the solution carefully.

4. Add the laundry bluing to the solution. Stir the solution carefully—without spilling—until the solution is evenly mixed and the salt is completely dissolved.

5. Write your names on the tray and place a wad of 4 or 5 white facial tissues in the tray.

6. Carefully pour the solution over the tissues in the tray.

7. Place the tray in hot, direct sunlight or in a warm place until the solution dries. It will usually take a day or two.

8. Sketch what your garden looks like after a couple of days:

 NAME _____

CREATING CRYSTAL GARDENS

CREATING A SPECTACULAR CRYSTAL GARDEN *(cont.)*

This activity is a variation of your garden from the previous page. You will use the same types of materials except for one—the kind of salt used. Rock salt is a hard kind of salt with much larger crystals than table salt. It is sometimes used to insulate cold foods and to melt snow and ice. It will take much longer to dissolve rock salt in the water. It may also take much longer for the crystals to form.

Directions: Work in teams of two as you perform these activities. Gather these materials as directed by your teacher.

> ### TEAM MATERIALS
> - $\frac{1}{2}$ ounce of ammonia
> - 1 ounce (30 cc) rock salt
> - 1 ounce (30 mL) of laundry bluing
> - 1 ounce (30 mL) of warm water
> - 6- or 8-ounce clear plastic cup
>
> - facial tissues
> - flat polystyrene foam tray or bowl
> - food coloring (optional)
> - straw or stirrer

Directions

1. Pour the water into the 8-oz. plastic cup. Add food coloring, if desired.

2. Pour the rock salt into the water and stir until all or nearly all of the salt is dissolved.

3. Pour in the ammonia. Stir the solution carefully.

4. Add the laundry bluing to the solution. Stir the solution carefully without spilling and until the solution is evenly mixed and the salt is completely dissolved.

5. Write your names on the tray and place a wad of 4 or 5 white facial tissues in the tray.

6. Carefully pour the solution over the tissues in the tray.

7. Place the tray in hot, direct sunlight or in a warm place until the solution dries. It will usually take a day or two.

8. Sketch your setup in the box.

You will have time to examine and compare the crystal gardens in the next activity.

CREATING CRYSTAL GARDENS

JOURNAL ENTRY

1. Which crystal garden (salt crystal, stalagmites and stalactites, or "fancy crystals") that you made was most impressive? Why? Describe the features of the garden.

   _____

   _____

   _____

2. What changes or improvements would you have made to any of the gardens you created?

   _____

   _____

   _____

3. Were there any ingredients or materials in the formulas that were the same for all of the crystal activities?

   _____

   _____

   _____

4. At this point in your studies, which crystal material seemed to make the best gardens? Why?

   _____

   _____

   _____

5. What formula or combination of materials would you like to try if you were designing your own crystal garden?

   _____

   _____

   _____

DESIGN PROCESS REVIEW—CREATING CRYSTAL GARDENS

Share your journal entries and general observations with your classmates in a discussion led by your teacher.

BECOME A CRYSTAL SCULPTOR

CHALLENGE ACTIVITY

Your Salt Garden Crystal Formation—Final Examination (Date: _____)

Examine the crystal solution that you poured on the coal, rocks, and tissues. Use a magnifying glass. Try not to disturb the crystals.

EXAMINING YOUR "FANCY CRYSTAL" TRAY—FINAL EXAMINATION

Use your magnifying glass to examine the crystals.

1. Which material—the string, the swab, or the paper towel—has the most crystals? Why do you think it has the most crystals?

   _____

   _____

2. What color and shape are the crystals?

   _____

3. Are there crystals on the tray itself? Has all of the water evaporated from the tray?

   _____

4. Separate a single crystal from the others. What features do you notice about this crystal? What geometric figure does it most resemble? Have the crystals changed since the last examination?

   _____

   _____

YOUR STALAGMITE AND STALACTITE GARDENS—FINAL EXAMINATION

Reexamine your crystal formation grown with washing soda. Look at the shapes of the structures formed, the colors of the structures, and the individual crystals. Use your magnifying glass.

1. What are the basic shape or shapes of the large formation now? Describe the general look of the formation. Has it changed or remained the same? Did a hard shell of crystals form on top of the cups?

   _____

   _____

2. Examine individual crystals. What crystal shapes can you see? Are the crystals small or large? What color are the crystals? Have these changed or remained the same since the last examination?

   _____

   _____

BECOME A CRYSTAL SCULPTOR

CHALLENGE ACTIVITY *(cont.)*

EXAMINING YOUR "FANCY CRYSTAL" TRAY—FINAL EXAMINATION

Use your magnifying glass to examine the crystals.

1. Which material—the string, the swab, or the paper towel—now has the most crystals? Why, do you think, it has the most crystals?

_____

2. What color and shape are the crystals? Have they changed?

_____

3. Separate a single crystal from the others. What do you notice about this crystal? What geometric figure does it most resemble?

_____

4. What substance did you use to make these crystals?

_____

YOUR SPECTACULAR CRYSTAL GARDEN AND SPECTACULAR ROCK CRYSTAL GARDEN

1. Examine your spectacular crystal gardens and rock crystal gardens. Describe the colors, shapes, and the general way the crystals have grown and spread.

_____

2. What, do you think, created the difference in this garden?

_____

3. Sketch crystals from the table salt crystal garden and rock salt crystal garden in the boxes below.

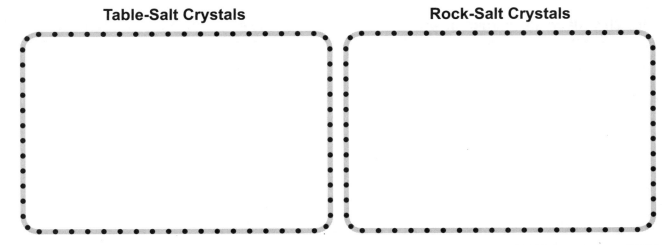

Table-Salt Crystals	Rock-Salt Crystals

 **NAME** _____

BECOME A CRYSTAL SCULPTOR

CHALLENGE ACTIVITY—DESIGN YOUR OWN CRYSTAL GARDEN

Directions: Use the Design Process Worksheet on page 5 to help guide you through the process. Create a crystal garden by using the materials listed below.

1. You may use up to 1 ounce, 30 mL, or 30 cc of any (or all) of these crystal-creating materials listed below:
   - table salt
   - rock salt
   - sugar
   - washing soda
2. You may use up to 2 oz. or 60 mL of water.
3. You may use up to 15 mL of ammonia.
4. You may use up to 15 mL of vinegar.
5. You may use up to 15 mL of bluing.
6. You may use string, tissue, rocks, or other materials for your crystals to grow on.

YOUR FORMULA:

Describe your setup and the steps you followed when you were creating your crystal garden.

_____

_____

_____

What results did you expect?

_____

_____

What results did you get?

_____

_____

Sketch your crystal garden below, after allowing a few days to pass for crystals to form.

BECOME A CRYSTAL SCULPTOR

CHALLENGE ACTIVITY—JOURNAL ENTRY

Use a computer, tablet, or other device to answer each paragraph subject below. Be sure to use paragraph format and complete sentences.

PARAGRAPH 1

How would you build or create a crystal garden for your parents or younger siblings?

Provide explicit details in terms of materials used, the amounts of materials (even water), and the process of adding or combining materials. (You may refer to your activity notes.)

PARAGRAPH 2

How long would the crystal garden last? What could you do to make it last longer?

PARAGRAPH 3

Describe what you think the crystal garden would look like in terms of colors and shapes.

PARAGRAPH 4

Describe and explain what you learned from doing this project in several sentences.

How successful was your own crystal garden invention?

PARAGRAPH 5

Respond to these questions by referring back to the activities you completed in this unit.

1. *How are crystals formed?*
2. *What materials contain crystals?*
3. *Which materials and methods make the best crystals?*
4. *How are all crystals alike?*
5. *How do crystals differ in size, shape, and color?*

DESIGN PROCESS REVIEW—BECOME A CRYSTAL GARDEN SCULPTOR

Share your crystal garden and experiences with your classmates in the class discussion/presentation your teacher leads to culminate the unit.

GO FLY A KITE

4 Sessions: 1 session per each activity (approximately 1 to $1\frac{1}{2}$ hours per session)

CONNECTIONS AND SUGGESTIONS

SCIENCE—Students will explore the forces of lift, drag, and gravity by constructing kites of different shapes and testing them.

TECHNOLOGY—Students will use the materials listed in the lesson to create flying apparatuses with specific technological functions. For this project, students will use basic computer software to write a brief report in which they describe the problems encountered, the solutions attempted, the success rate of each activity, the different approaches used, and any suggestions for improvement.

ENGINEERING—Students will experiment with a variety of engineering designs and the listed materials to create kites to test their skill and ability to follow directions. They will also have an opportunity to improve on the basic designs.

MATH—Students will use their measurement and estimation skills for judging distances and creating kites as directed.

Materials

- colored tissue paper
- empty spools (smooth cylindrical wooden sticks, dowels, or empty paper-towel rolls will work)
- fishing line (8-pound test or above is easier for students—and adults—to manipulate)
- kite string (several rolls)
- pencils

- plastic rings or plastic buttons with large holes
- plastic stirrers or straws
- rulers
- scissors
- tape (masking and clear)
- yardstick or meterstick

UNIT 2 VOCABULARY

air resistance—the force of air moving against an object such as a kite

bridle—the lines attached to the kite that help direct its movement

cell (of a kite)—one compartment of a kite (usually made of fabric or paper)

cross spar—the part of a kite frame that runs horizontal across the kite

cube—a square three-dimensional geometric shape with the same length, width, and height

diagonal—a slanting line between opposite corners

drag—the force on an object that resists its motion

equilateral—a figure with equal sides

equilibrium—a state of balance between two weights or forces

flying line—the string used to pull the kite through the air

lift—upward pressure that air exerts on a kite (or aircraft), counteracting the force of gravity

notch—a V- or U-shaped cut

sail—the material (usually cloth or paper) that a kite is made from (excluding the frame)

spar—the frame of a kite (usually wooden)

spine—the long, vertical part of the inner frame

spool—the piece of round wood or other material that holds the kite string

tail (of the kite)—the bits of paper, fabric, or plastic tied to the bottom of the kite's frame

tetrahedron—a solid figure with four equal triangular faces

DISCUSSION PROMPT:

Kites are fun for sport and recreation, but did you know that kites have had many practical uses over the years? In 13th-century China, they were used to provide wind power with which to propel canoes. During the American Civil War, they were used for delivering letters and newspapers. In Indonesia, kites are still used for fishing. What other uses do you think kites might have had, or will have in the future?

GO FLY A KITE

A kite is a form of aircraft consisting of one or more wings connected to a system that anchors it (such as a person holding the string). A kite is capable of flight because faster-moving air flowing above the surface of the wing (kite) produces low pressure above the wing and higher pressure is thus exerted below the wing. This combination of forces creates *lift*—the movement of the kite into the air. Kites need some air movement or wind to create this combination of pressures and lift.

The movement of the kite also creates a horizontal *drag* in the direction of the wing. The force created by towing the kite—from the *bridle* and the *flying line*—works with the forces of drag and lift to allow the kite to take flight.

Kites were an invention first made in China about 25 centuries ago, where bamboo provided a light, strong frame, and silk provided a light, strong fabric for covering the kite.

The tetrahedral kite was invented by Alexander Graham Bell, the creator of the first practical telephone. He made very large versions of the kite with wood and fabric. He even designed and built a boat in the tetrahedral shape. This kite is made from tetrahedral-shaped cells. A tetrahedral kite is easy to construct, very durable in high winds, and can be made quite large. It is a little hard to get flying in light winds but very easy to keep airborne.

Use a computer or tablet to search for information on the Internet to help you as you complete the activities in this unit. Helpful search items include:

air flow	bridle	spar	tetrahedral kite
air pressure	diamond kite	strut	wing
anchor	drag	tensile	
box kite	lift	tether	

BUILD A DIAMOND KITE

Directions: Work in teams of two as you perform this activity. Gather these materials as directed by your teacher.

> ## TEAM MATERIALS
> - colored tissue paper
> - empty spools (smooth cylindrical wooden sticks, dowels, or empty paper towel rolls will work)
> - fishing line (8- to 20-pound test)
>
> - kite string
> - plastic rings or buttons with large holes
> - rulers
> - scissors
>
> - straight plastic straws or stirrers
> - tape (masking or clear)
> - yardstick (or meterstick)

GETTING STARTED

Successful kites are produced by careful, accurate work and specific measurements. Effective construction is produced by the following actions:

- Make the knots for the kites very tight.
- Use enough paper to overlap the faces that make up the sail of the kite.
- Make sure you tape all the paper ends firmly and carefully.
- Make careful measurements.
- Make sure the kite is not so long, wide, or tall that it could be slowed down by air resistance, weight, or size.
- Careful workmanship counts. Pay attention to even the smallest details.

MAKING THE DIAMOND FRAME

1. You will make the inner frame of the diamond kite first. Make a slit 1 inch long in one end of one plastic straw. Make an identical slit on the same end of the straw but on the opposite side.

2. Slip the split end of the straw into the end of another straw of the same size. Use one strip of masking tape to make the connection firm. This is the long part of the inner frame of the kite and is called the *spine*.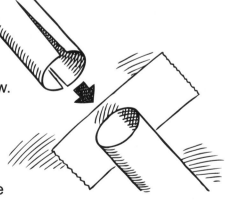

3. Make a slit 2 inches long in one end of another plastic straw. Make an identical slit on the same end of the straw but on the opposite side.

4. Slip the split end of the straw into the end of another straw of the same size. Use one strip of masking tape to make this connection firm. This is the horizontal part of the frame called the *cross spar*.

5. Use the two pieces you have made in order to create the inner frame of the kite. Measure 3 inches down the longer piece (the spine). Lay the cross spar over the spine.

6. Use a thin strip of tape to firmly connect the pieces in the form of the cross.

_____

Build a Diamond Kite

Adding the Outer Frame

Use six straws to create the outer frame.

1. Connect two straws by slitting the end of one straw and placing this end into another straw and then taping the ends in place. Connect two more straws the same way. They will form the rear of the kite.

2. Arrange the straws in a diamond shape with the two unconnected straws as the head and the two pairs of connected straws as the rear.

3. Run a long piece of fishing line through the six straws, and tie it firmly in a diamond shape (shorter straws in front).

4. Lay the diamond over the inner frame. Use small strips of masking tape to connect the four points of contact: the nose, the two wingtips, and then the rear. It should be sturdy but not heavy.

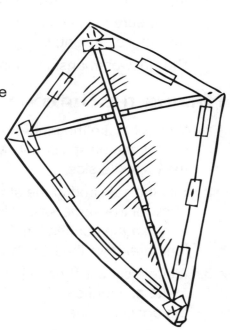

Covering the Frame

1. Lay a piece of colored tissue paper flat on a desk.

2. Center the frame on top of the paper so that all parts of the frame are inside the edges of the paper.

3. Fold the paper over the frame neatly and use clear tape or masking tape to attach the paper to the frame so that the back of the kite is also covered (or nearly covered). Make sure there are no large openings where air can get inside the paper. This is the **sail** of the kite.

BUILD A DIAMOND KITE

MAKING THE TAIL

1. Cut six pieces of tissue paper to be about 3 inches long and 1 inch wide.

2. Tie a piece of 18- to 24-inch-long fishing line to the rear of the kite.

3. Tie each piece of tissue paper about 2 inches apart to the fishing line.

4. This creates a tail for the kite. It acts as a rudder and provides stability.

MAKING THE BRIDLE

The kite bridle is the arrangement of strings between the kite and the flying line. It holds the kite at an angle and affects how the kite flies.

1. Use a piece of fishing line to create the bridle.

2. Cut the line about 3 to 4 inches longer than the length of the spine.

3. Tie one end of the fishing line firmly to the top of the spine.

4. Slide a plastic ring or a plastic button with big holes onto the line. If there is a gap in the ring, be sure to tape it up so the line doesn't slip out.

5. Tie the fishing line to the rear of the spine, leaving this bridle line loose.

GO FLY A KITE

You will need a fairly strong and steady breeze to fly your kite. Make sure you have plenty of space away from obstructions such as poles, trees, or buildings.

1. Tie one end of the kite string to the bridle ring so that the ring is loose and easily moved.

2. Make sure the kite string is attached to a spool or cylindrical piece of wood (like a smooth stick, a dowel, or even an empty paper-towel roll) in your hand and that it unwinds easily. (You will need to wind the string around the spool before you attempt to fly your kite. This helps keep it from tangling.)

3. Face into the breeze and run into the wind, letting string out as the wind catches the kite.

4. With your partner, take turns running into the wind while your partner tosses the kite high enough for the wind to catch it.

 _____

BUILD A DIAMOND KITE

MAKING ADJUSTMENTS

After you and your partner have tested your kite a few times, make the following adjustments to see if it helps your kite fly more efficiently. Check off each step as you complete it.

☐ Check for loose tape, holes, and flapping paper. Tape down any loose paper that is on the body of the kite.

☐ Make sure all strings are tied. Use double knots for added strength.

☐ Make sure your kite line comes smoothly and easily off the spool.

☐ Use one hand to hold the spool and the other to hold the kite string in the air.

☐ Make sure the weight of the kite body is even on both sides of the frame. Add extra straws and/or tape to the lighter side, if needed.

☐ Make sure the bridle ring moves freely.

☐ Try hooking the bridle to the cross spar as well as the spine.

☐ If the frame is coming apart, use extra straws to reinforce the damaged kite.

EVALUATE YOUR KITE

On the lines below, list what worked well on your kite.

1. _____

2. _____

3. _____

4. _____

5. _____

On the lines below, describe problems you encountered.

1. _____

2. _____

3. _____

4. _____

5. _____

BUILD A DIAMOND KITE

JOURNAL ENTRY

1. Describe the solutions you would use—or did use—to solve one or more problems you had with your kite.

_____

_____

_____

_____

2. What was the hardest part of this science activity?

_____

_____

_____

_____

3. What improvement would you make to the kite design? What problem would it solve?

_____

_____

_____

_____

4. Would the kite work better if it were bigger? How? Why?

_____

_____

_____

_____

DESIGN PROCESS REVIEW—MAKING A DIAMOND KITE

Share your journal entries and experiences with your class during a discussion moderated by your teacher.

 NAME _____

BUILD A BOX KITE

Directions: Work in teams of two as you perform this activity. Gather these materials as directed by your teacher.

TEAM MATERIALS

- colored tissue paper
- empty spools (smooth cylindrical wooden sticks, dowels, or empty paper-towel rolls will work)
- fishing line (8- to 20-pound test)
- kite string
- pencils

- plastic rings or buttons that have large holes
- rulers
- scissors
- straight plastic straws
- tape (masking or clear)
- yardstick (or meterstick)

GETTING STARTED

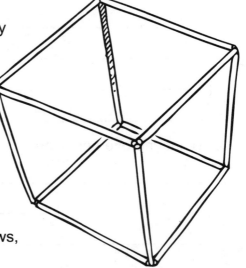

1. Thread a 36-inch piece of fishing line through four sturdy plastic straws. (Thin stirrer straws will work, but they are harder to thread.)

2. Tie a knot connecting the straws. (Always tie twice to keep the figure sturdy.)

3. Tie about 28 inches of fishing line to a corner of the square, thread the line through three more straws, and tie it to the closest corner.

4. Tie another piece of fishing line about 28 inches long to an open corner, thread the line through three more straws, and tie it down at the corner next to it.

5. Tie a piece of fishing line about 12 inches long to the top of one of the upright straws, feed it through one empty straw, and tie it to the top of the upright straw next to it. This will connect the two upright squares on one side.

6. Do the same with the last straw so that you have formed a cube made of 12 straws.

(Make sure all the knots are tight and firm. Use extra fishing line to strengthen any loose connections. The cube will lean a little bit at this point until the kite is completed.)

MAKING THE SECOND CUBE

1. Repeat the directions for the cube above.

2. Make sure all knots are firmly tied in double knots.

3. If needed, use extra fishing line to retie loose straws.

BUILD A BOX KITE

CONNECTING THE CUBES

1. You will need four straws and four pieces of fishing line, each about 1 foot long. Tie one end of each piece of fishing line to one square corner of one cube.

2. Thread one straw through a fishing line, and tie the line to the corresponding corner of the other cube.

3. Thread each string through a straw, and tie each string off so that there are three cubes lined in a row.

MAKING THE KITE STRONGER—DIAGONAL REINFORCEMENT

To improve your kite's flying capability, it is best to reinforce each box with a diagonal strut:

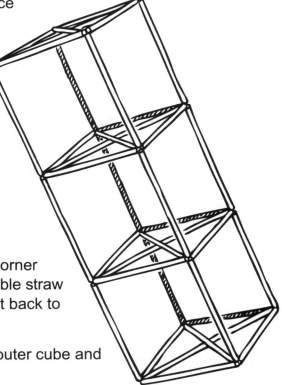

1. Slit a new straw to about 1 inch from the end.

2. Slide the slit end of the straw into another straw and tape it in place.

3. Cut a piece of fishing line about 16 inches long.

4. Tie one end of the fishing line to the corner of one of the outer cubes.

5. Feed the fishing line through the double straw you just made.

6. Tie the other end of the fishing line to the opposite corner of the cube to which you tied the first end. If the double straw is too long, remove it from the line, trim it to fit, add it back to the line, and tie it in place.

7. Attach at least one diagonal reinforcement to each outer cube and two reinforcements for the middle cube.

8. Face the reinforcements in different directions or cross them on one face of the cube.

BUILD A BOX KITE

COVERING THE FACES

You need to cover the first and last cube of your box kite with tissue paper.

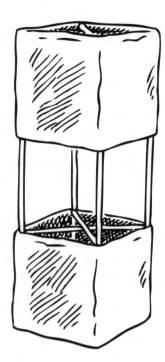

1. Lay the cube on a large piece of tissue paper about 8 inches wide and 33 inches long.

2. Wrap the tissue paper around one of the outer cubes, leaving the left and right side open.

3. Neatly tape the paper to the straw frame of the cube.

4. Lay the cube at the other end of the kite on another piece of tissue (8 by 33 inches) and tape it securely to this outer cube, leaving the left and right sides open.

NOTE: The center cube should be uncovered, as are both ends of the kite.

ATTACHING THE BRIDLE

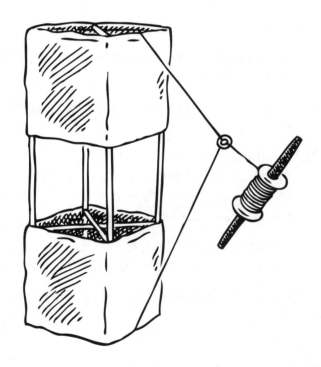

1. Cut two pieces of fishing line—one about 1 foot long and one about 2 feet long.

2. Tie the 2-foot-long piece to the first straw at the base of the cube at the far end of the kite.

3. Tie the 1-foot-long piece to the straw between the 2nd and 3rd cube at the base of nearest cube.

4. Use a plastic ring or a button that has large holes as a bridle ring. Make sure it won't let the fishing line slip out. (Tape it closed if it could let the fishing line slip out.)

5. Tie the end of each fishing line to the bridle ring. Make sure the knots are secure.

6. Tie one end of the kite string to the bridle ring and wrap the kite string around an empty spool (a cylindrical piece of wood or an empty paper-towel roll will also work).

BUILD A BOX KITE

FLYING YOUR BOX KITE

Work with your partner to launch the kite. One of you should hold the kite while the other holds the kite line/string.

1. Find an open playground, park, or field—away from power lines, large trees, and buildings.
2. Position the kite so that it faces into the wind. You will need a strong, steady breeze to fly the box kite.
3. Hold up the kite and gradually let out a little kite line as it catches the wind and begins to lift off.
4. Keep letting out line as the kite lifts higher into the air.
5. One partner may need to lift the kite and launch it into the air if the wind isn't strong enough at ground level.

BOX-KITE MODIFICATIONS

Ben Franklin's name and inventive nature have always been associated with kites. He used them in leisure moments, and he experimented with them to prove that lightning is a form of electricity, as well as to explore other scientific ideas.

As Mr. Franklin did, there are a number of variations you can do with your box kite to achieve better performance or different results. Try each of the following—one at a time—if your kite isn't performing as you wish or just to compare results.

1. Try covering the center cube with tissue paper. This may be helpful when the wind is steady but light and not too strong. The kite will be able to hold more air.
2. Make sure the weight of your kite is evenly balanced from one side to the other and top to bottom. If the kite has a tendency to flop over to one side, try using a few straws taped to the opposite side to achieve a balance of weight. Sometimes, a few pieces of tape will be enough to bring the balance into equilibrium.
3. If the straws are damaged or the paper is really torn, try mending them with small pieces of clear packing tape, which holds very well.
4. Sometimes the wind can be so strong that it can whip apart portions of the kite or can damage the straws by breaking them or blowing them loose. You can slit larger, wider straws and fit them over the damaged, thin straws. Tape these larger, stronger straws in place.
5. The bridle can be difficult to adjust or maneuver at times. If it lacks flexibility, try more elastic string or even kite string. Try using a different location for the plastic ring or bridle string.
6. Be a true scientist. Experiment with different materials, options, locations, and arrangements. Experiment . . . experiment . . . experiment . . . until it works.

BUILD A BOX KITE

JOURNAL ENTRY

1. What problems did you encounter in building your box kite?

   _____

   _____

   _____

2. When would you be most likely to use a box kite? What kind of weather, wind conditions, or time of year would be best?

   _____

   _____

   _____

3. What was the most tricky or difficult part of the box-kite construction? Why?

   _____

   _____

   _____

4. Which kite was the most successful, the box kite or the diamond kite? Explain your choice.

   _____

   _____

   _____

5. What information did you learn about nature from making and flying kites?

   _____

   _____

   _____

6. Why might a scientist or inventor experiment with kites?

   _____

   _____

   _____

DESIGN PROCESS REVIEW—BUILD A BOX KITE

Share your journal entries and experiences with your class during a discussion moderated by your teacher.

BUILD A TETRAHEDRAL KITE

Directions: Work in teams of two as you perform this activity. Gather these materials as directed by your teacher.

TEAM MATERIALS

- clear tape
- fishing line (8-pound test or higher)
- kite string
- paper-towel roll or cylindrical piece of wood

- plastic rings or buttons that have large holes
- scissors
- thin stirrer straws or regular straight straws
- tissue paper

GETTING STARTED

The simplest version of this kite is a one-cell model that flies, but it is so light that strong winds often just send it twirling. This cell is the basic unit of much larger tetrahedral kites. You will be using 4 cells to make a tetrahedral kite.

MAKING THE FIRST CELL

You need six straws or stirrers and four feet of fishing line for each cell. Thread the fishing line through three straws and tie it off in a triangle. Leave most of the fishing line on one end of the knot. Thread the rest of the line through two more straws and tie it off at one of the other corners of the first triangle. You now have a figure with two triangles.

Cut some fishing line and tie it to the tip of one of the triangles. Thread the line through a sixth straw and tie the line to the tip of the second triangle. Make sure all of the knots are tight. This forms a tetrahedron—a three-sided figure made with three equilateral triangles. The tetrahedron is an equilateral triangular prism.

COMPLETING THE KITE

1. Make three more cells the same way you made the first.

2. Make sure all of your knots are tight.

3. Arrange three of the cells as the base of the kite and tie them at the three corners where they touch another cell.

4. Arrange the fourth cell on top of the three cells so that you can tie it to the three tips of the base cells. This creates a tetrahedron again, with four equal sides.

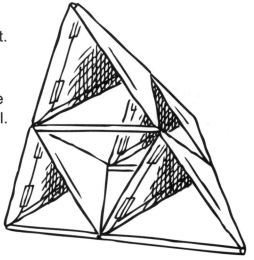

BUILD A TETRAHEDRAL KITE

COVERING THE CELLS

Wrap a strip of tissue paper so that it covers two faces of one tetrahedral cell. Fold a little extra over the straws and tape it securely to the frame and the inside of the paper.

Important:

- Each of the four cells needs to have two faces covered in the same way.
- Each of the four cells needs to have the bottom and front uncovered.

ATTACHING A BRIDLE

1. Cut two pieces of fishing line each about 1 foot (30 cm) long.
2. Tie one piece of fishing line to the tip of the top cell of the tetrahedron.
3. Tie the other piece of fishing line to the outside bottom tip of the tetrahedron so that the fishing lines are opposite each other along the outside ridge of the kite.
4. Place a plastic ring on the back of the tetrahedron at the bottom of the top cell.
5. Tie the ring to the top fishing line.
6. Tie the fishing line coming from the bottom cell to the ring as well. The ring will dangle about $\frac{2}{3}$ of the way down the spine of the tetrahedron.
7. Tie the kite string to the ring as well. Use a paper-towel roll or a cylindrical piece of wood as the spindle that holds your kite string.

FLYING THE TETRAHEDRAL KITE

This kite catches the wind well and flies, usually upside-down, for long distances. It works very well in a strong, steady breeze. Take your kite into an open field, lawn, park, or playground away from power lines, trees, and buildings. Face the kite into the wind and gradually let out your kite line. Pull the kite along into the wind until the breeze catches the kite and lifts it up into the air. If the wind doesn't catch it and lift it from ground level, you and your partner can also launch the kite by tossing it into the air.

Adjust the bridle if necessary. Some wind conditions require that the kite have a four-legged bridle with two more fishing lines connected to each of the other corners of the kite and the ring.

BUILD A TETRAHEDRAL KITE

JOURNAL ENTRY

1. What was the most difficult part of building your tetrahedral kite?

   _____

   _____

   _____

   _____

2. What difficulty did you have in flying the kite?

   _____

   _____

   _____

3. How high did your kite fly?

   _____

   _____

   _____

   _____

4. Did your kite twirl when strong, gusty breezes were blowing? Could you stabilize the kite? What did you do?

   _____

   _____

   _____

   _____

5. What kind of wind or breeze was best for flying this kite? Explain your answer.

   _____

   _____

   _____

   _____

DESIGN PROCESS REVIEW—BUILD A TETRAHEDRAL KITE

Share your journal entries and experiences with your class during a discussion moderated by your teacher.

DESIGN YOUR OWN KITE

CHALLENGE ACTIVITY—DESIGN YOUR OWN KITE

TEAM MATERIALS

- stirrers or straws
- fishing line (8-pound test or higher)
- scissors
- tissue paper
- clear adhesive tape
- masking tape

TRY THIS—THINK BIG

Alexander Graham Bell made his tetrahedral kites very large. You can also make and fly much larger kites. To make yours larger, add a third layer onto your original tetrahedral kite by using six cells. Make each cell from six straws as before. Make six cells, and connect them in a triangle shape in one layer. Make sure each cell is connected and tied to every adjoining cell.

Set your original four-cell tetrahedral kite on top of your new base. Use fishing line to attach it carefully on top of your six-cell addition. You now have a three-level tetrahedral kite. It should work very well in the air as long as you have a good breeze and have checked all of your knots.

GO SUPER SIZED

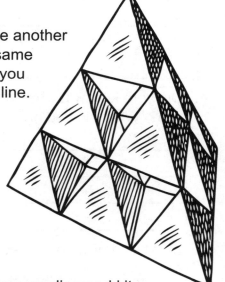

You may want to connect with another pair of partners and create another layer for your kite. This layer has 10 cells. Each are made the same way as before. Arrange the 10 cells in a triangular formation as you did the three- and six-cell bases. Tie the cells firmly with fishing line.

Set your three-layer kite on top of this fourth layer. Attach the bottom cells to the upper layer as you did before. Check your bridle connections.

Carry your super-sized tetrahedral kite to your favorite flight area for a test flight when the wind is strong.

OTHER KITE POSSIBILITIES

- You may choose to create a longer box kite or a larger or stronger diamond kite. You may want to create your own design. Make sure it's a good aerodynamic design, capable of catching the air and riding the wind.
- Work with other groups and combine 10 of the original 6-cell tetrahedral kites in the class to make one giant kite.

DESIGN YOUR OWN KITE

CHALLENGE ACTIVITY—DESIGN PROCESS

Describe and illustrate your design below. (You may also use the Design Process Worksheet on page 5 to help you.)

Explain the procedure for making this kite:

_____

_____

_____

_____

_____

Draw an illustration of your kite here.

DESIGN YOUR OWN KITE

CHALLENGE ACTIVITY—JOURNAL ENTRY

Use a computer, tablet, or other device to answer each paragraph subject below. Be sure to use paragraph format and complete sentences.

PARAGRAPH 1

What was the most difficult part of building your tetrahedral kite? Explain the difficulties.

PARAGRAPH 2

Which tetrahedral size worked best for your team? Why? How big did you want to build the kite? How many cells did you use in all?

PARAGRAPH 3

How did your tetrahedral kite react in gentle breezes and in strong winds? Which air movement was most effective in flying this kite?

PARAGRAPH 4

Alexander Graham Bell built a boat in the shape of a tetrahedron. Do you think this shape could have helped move a boat through the water? How? Would you like to ride in a boat of that shape?

PARAGRAPH 5

Respond to these questions by referring back to the activities you completed in this unit.

1. *How can you make a diamond kite?*
2. *How high can you fly the kite on a day that has moderate wind?*
3. *Which style of kite works best in moderate and strong winds?*
4. *How do you make and fly a box kite?*
5. *Which style of kite is the easiest to get airborne and keep flying?*

DESIGN PROCESS REVIEW—DESIGN YOUR OWN KITE

Share your kite and experiences with your classmates in the class discussion/presentations your teacher leads to culminate the unit.

STATIC ELECTRICITY

4 Sessions: 1 session per each activity (approximately 1 to $1\frac{1}{2}$ hours per session)

CONNECTIONS AND SUGGESTIONS

SCIENCE—Students will explore the properties of static electricity—creating and using static charges.

TECHNOLOGY—Students will use computers or tablets to record and report on the results of these static-electricity investigations. They can record results on charts they create. They will do a final journal entry and respond to testable questions posed in the introduction to the unit.

ENGINEERING—The engineering in these activities involves design features that facilitate the creation of static charges. Students can observe the effects of these static charges.

MATH—Most of the math in this unit involves timing the length that a static charge is held by various materials and determining the amount of material that a charge attracts.

Materials

- aluminum foil
- balloons of various shapes and sizes
- black pepper
- cinnamon
- fishing line, thin string, or thread
- grass seeds
- large sheets of paper, such as colored construction paper
- oregano

- parsley
- ruler
- scissors
- small bits of dried leaves and grass
- small pieces of cotton
- stopwatch/watch/clock
- table salt
- white facial tissue/bits of tissue paper
- white paper

UNIT 3 VOCABULARY

attract—to draw toward an object

conductor—a material that allows electrons or an electrical current to flow easily (electrons move freely in an electrical current)

current—the flow of an electric charge carried along by moving electrons in a conductor, such as a wire from a source of electricity (such as a battery) to a use for electricity (such as lighting a bulb)

discharge—the release of static electricity through a gas, liquid, or solid

electromagnetism—one of the four fundamental forces holding the universe together

electron—a particle circling an atom, carrying a negative charge

electroscope—an early scientific instrument used to detect the presence of an electric charge or to measure it

electrostatic discharge—the release of static electricity when two objects come into contact (such as when you touch metal after shuffling your feet on carpet)

inflate—to fill with air or gas

neutron—a particle in the nucleus of an atom that has no charge

particles—bits of matter or parts of atoms—includes particles with positive charges (protons) or negative charges (electrons)

proton—a particle with a positive charge in the nucleus of an atom

repel—to thrust or push away from an object

static electricity—a build up of electric charges on the surface of a material—the charge remains until it can move away either by electric current or electrical discharge

DISCUSSION PROMPT:

We've all felt that painful, frustrating *ZAP* when we've walked across a carpet and reached for a metal door handle. Or we've pulled off our hat only to discover our hair is standing straight up from our head! Static electricity can often be annoying (if not painful), but there are ways to help eliminate it. Increasing the humidity in your home helps, as dry air increases the frequency of shocks. In the same way, spritzing water on your hair helps reduce the static electricity. Dryer sheets thrown in the dryer coat clothes with a conductive substance that keeps them from having "static cling." There are even anti-static hand lotions! What else have you found to help reduce static electricity?

STATIC ELECTRICITY

There are no wires nor continuous flow of electricity in static electricity. Instead, static electricity is created by rubbing certain materials against each other. For example, materials such as rubber, plastic, or glass rubbed against hair, silk, wool, some other types of cloth, and similar materials can create static electricity. Because these materials do not conduct electricity easily, the rubbing tends to build up and maintain a static charge for a short time.

All physical objects are made up of atoms. Within each tiny atom are three smaller kinds of particles: protons, neutrons, and electrons. Protons are positively charged. Neutrons are neutral (they have no charge). Electrons are negatively charged.

Opposite charges attract. Like charges repel. Most of the time, positive and negative charges carried by protons and electrons are balanced within an object. Static electricity occurs when the charges are not in balance. Rubbing certain objects together transfers electrons from one object to another. For example, rubbing a balloon on your clothes transfers a surplus of electrons to the balloon. A wall—which would be more positively charged than the balloon in comparison—would then attract the balloon, causing it to stick to the wall. The same thing happens when you rub your shoes against a rug. This creates a static charge when you touch a cat or dog. Your pet may have some raised hair for a while.

Use a computer or tablet to search for information on the Internet to help you as you complete the activities in this unit. Helpful search items include:

| electric charge | neutrons | protons |
| electric current | electrons | static discharge |

PEPPER PICKER-UPPER

Directions: Work in teams of two as you perform this first activity. Gather these materials as directed by your teacher.

TEAM MATERIALS

- balloons of various shapes and sizes
- black pepper
- ruler
- white paper (or paper plate)

1. Spread about three pinches of pepper on a piece of white paper or paper plate. Inflate a small balloon, such as one used for water balloons. Tie it off and rub the balloon **one way only** through your hair 10 times. (Do not rub back-and-forth for the first two tests.) Hold the balloon about 12 inches (30 cm) above the pepper. Use a ruler to measure the distance.

   Did you attract any pepper to the balloon? _____

   Clean the balloon, rub it again the same way, and lower the balloon to 6 inches, then 3 inches. What results did you get? Record how much pepper your balloon picked up: ALL, MOST, SOME, or NONE.

RESULTS AT 12 INCHES	RESULTS AT 6 INCHES	RESULTS AT 3 INCHES

2. Do the experiment again, but rub the balloon 20 times this time—**one way only**. Hold the balloon 12 inches above the table with the pepper. (Use a ruler to measure the distances.) Record how much pepper your balloon picked up. Test again at 6 and 3 inches.

RESULTS AT 12 INCHES	RESULTS AT 6 INCHES	RESULTS AT 3 INCHES

3. Try the experiment this time by rubbing the balloon **back and forth** across your hair. Hold the balloon 12 inches above the table that has the pepper. Record how much pepper your balloon picked up. Clean the balloon, rub it again, and lower it to 6 inches, then 3 inches. What results did you get? Record how much pepper your balloon picked up.

RESULTS AT 12 INCHES	RESULTS AT 6 INCHES	RESULTS AT 3 INCHES

4. Why do you think you didn't pick up as much pepper when you rubbed your hair back and forth? What did you do that was different?

   _____

   _____

   _____

PEPPER PICKER-UPPER

5. Replace the pepper and inflate a **long balloon**. Do the experiment again. Be sure to rub the length of the balloon against your hair. Rub 10 times in **one direction only**. Record the results below. Test again at 6 inches and 3 inches.

RESULTS AT 12 INCHES	RESULTS AT 6 INCHES	RESULTS AT 3 INCHES

6. Now rub 20 times—**one way only**. Record your results for 20 rubbings.

RESULTS AT 12 INCHES	RESULTS AT 6 INCHES	RESULTS AT 3 INCHES

7. Replace the pepper and inflate a **large, round balloon**. Rub the balloon against your hair 10 times—**one way only**. Record the results below.

RESULTS AT 12 INCHES	RESULTS AT 6 INCHES	RESULTS AT 3 INCHES

8. Rub the large, round balloon 20 times against your hair—**one way only**. Record the results.

RESULTS AT 12 INCHES	RESULTS AT 6 INCHES	RESULTS AT 3 INCHES

9. Which balloon carried the best static charge and thus picked up the most pepper?

_____

10. What advantage did the long balloon have over the small balloons? Why was it able to pick up a lot of pepper?

_____

_____

11. Did the round balloon work as well as the long one or the small one? _____

12. What advantage does the size of the round balloon give it in picking up the pepper?

_____

_____

13. What did the static electricity produce by rubbing your hair or your partner's hair?

_____

_____

 **NAME** _____

PEPPER PICKER-UPPER

JOURNAL ENTRY

1. The static electricity produced by rubbing hair is the force that picked up the pepper flakes. Where and when have you seen static electricity at home or at school?

   _____

   _____

   _____

2. What other items besides pepper could you pick up by rubbing a balloon?

   _____

   _____

   _____

3. Why do you think a balloon worked but a paperback book would probably not work?

   _____

   _____

   _____

4. What other materials besides a balloon might hold a static charge? Why?

   _____

   _____

   _____

5. What other materials or things might produce a static charge when rubbed by a balloon?

   _____

   _____

   _____

DESIGN PROCESS REVIEW—PEPPER PICKER-UPPER

Share your journal entries and experiences with your class during a discussion moderated by your teacher.

BALLOONS ON THE WALL

Directions:

1. Blow up and tie one **long balloon**. Rub the balloon **one way only** over your hair. Rub it over your hair front-to-back and then rub it again front-to-back. Repeat this for about 10 rubbings.

2. Place the balloon on a wall in the classroom. Time how long the balloon remains on the wall before falling.

   How many seconds before it fell? _____

3. Rub the balloon on your hair again. Use 20 rubbings this time. Place the balloon on a wall in the classroom. Time how long the balloon remains on the wall before falling.

   How many seconds before it fell? _____

   Was this longer than your first effort? _____

4. Rub the balloon against your shirt, jeans, or another article of clothing. Rub in **one direction only**. Rub 10 times and place the balloon on the wall again.

   Time how long the balloon remains on the wall before the balloon falls.

   How many seconds before it fell?

   _____

   Rub the balloon 20 times on your clothes and place it on the wall. Time how long it stayed on the wall.

   How many seconds before it fell?

   _____

NAME _____

BALLOONS ON THE WALL

TRIALS

Directions: Complete the trials listed below with the long balloon and record the times in seconds and minutes for each experiment.

CHARTING RESULTS—TECHNOLOGY PROCEDURE

Use a computer to make a table like the one below.

1. Open **Word** or **Google Docs**.
2. Click on the **Table** and insert a table. You will need to fill in how many rows and columns you need.

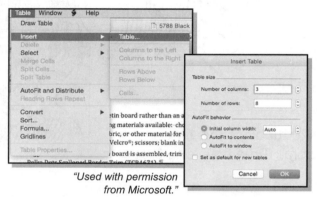

"Used with permission from Microsoft."

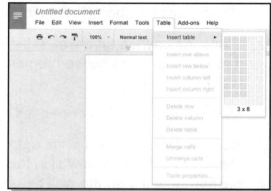

©2015 Google Inc, used with permission. Google and the Google logo are registered trademarks of Google Inc.

3. The table should have 3 columns and 8 rows.
4. Your empty table will appear on your page.
5. You can make adjustments by going back to **Table** on the menu bar. You can make the size of the cells different, and you can add or delete rows and columns.
6. Label the table and fill it in with the results of testing your balloon. Add any notes and observations that you made while testing.

LONG BALLOON		
MATERIAL RUBBED	**# TIMES RUBBED**	**TIME ON THE WALL (MIN./SEC.)**
1. hair	20	
2. jeans/pants	20	
3. shirt	20	
4. friend's hair	20	
5. down one arm	20	
6. shoe	20	

Which material was best for creating a static charge? Why? _____

_____

Test some other materials from the classroom, your desks, your backpacks, and the closet. Create a table like the one above listing the materials and whether they had **no attraction**, **some attraction**, or **strong attraction**.

BALLOONS ON THE WALL

TESTING OTHER BALLOONS

Try a different balloon shape or size. Record your results below.

BALLOON SHAPE: _____

MATERIAL RUBBED	# TIMES RUBBED	TIME ON THE WALL (MIN./SEC.)
1. hair	20	
2. jeans/pants	20	
3. shirt	20	
4. friend's hair	20	
5. down one arm	20	
6. shoe	20	

Try your favorite balloon shape. Describe your balloon and record your results in the table.

BALLOON SHAPE: _____

MATERIAL RUBBED	# TIMES RUBBED	TIME ON THE WALL (MIN./SEC.)
1. hair	20	
2. jeans/pants	20	
3. shirt	20	
4. friend's hair	20	
5. down one arm	20	
6. shoe	20	

BALLOONS ON THE WALL

JOURNAL ENTRY

1. Which type of hair worked best? Did it make a difference if it was short hair, long hair, curly hair, fine hair, or thick hair? Did it help if there was some type of product (hairspray or gel) in the hair?

   _____

   _____

   _____

2. How did the shape of the balloon affect its ability to stick to the wall? Did the balloon need a large surface area in order to stick to the wall?

   _____

   _____

   _____

3. What did you learn that you didn't know before this experiment?

   _____

   _____

   _____

4. How could you use at home what you learned from this activity?

   _____

   _____

   _____

5. Where have you seen static electricity working at home or school?

   _____

   _____

DESIGN PROCESS REVIEW—BALLOONS ON THE WALL

Share your journal entries and experiences with your class during a discussion moderated by your teacher.

STATIC PICK-UPS

Directions: Work in teams of two as you perform this activity. Gather these materials as directed by your teacher.

> **TEAM MATERIALS**
> - balloons of different shapes and sizes
> - cinnamon
> - clock or stopwatch
> - grass seeds
> - large sheets of paper, such as colored construction paper
> - oregano
> - parsley
> - pepper
> - small bits of dried leaves and grass
> - small pieces of cotton
> - table salt

UNPEPPERING THE SALT

1. Blow up a balloon of any size or shape. Choose one that you found worked well in previous experiments for producing and holding a static charge.

2. Spread some salt onto a piece of paper.

3. Rub the balloon along your hair **one way only** 10 times.

4. Hold the balloon a few inches above the salt. Describe the results. How much salt, if any, did the balloon attract? Could you hear it being picked up by the balloon?

   _____

5. Wipe the salt off the balloon so it falls back onto the paper. Try the experiment again using a different material on which to rub the balloon, such as a friend's longer hair, the length of a pair of jeans, or a wider piece of material. What were the results this time with 10 rubbings?

   _____

   _____

6. Do the same experiment with 20 rubbings. What happened to the salt?

   _____

   _____

7. Stir some black pepper in with the salt on the paper. Rub the balloon 20 times again. Could you "unpepper" the salt by lifting the pepper from the salt? Describe what happened.

   _____

   _____

   _____

STATIC PICK-UPS

UNPEPPERING THE SALT *(cont.)*

8. Stir in some other herbs and spices—such as oregano, cinnamon, or parsley—into your salt-and-pepper mixture. Rub your balloon 20 times on your favorite hair or material. What were you able to pick up?

    _____

    _____

9. Tear one tissue into small pieces that are each about an inch long. Place a layer of tissue next to the inch-long pieces. Rub your balloon on your hair or your favorite material for creating a static charge. Do 20 rubbings—one way only. What pieces did it pick up? Describe your results.

    _____

    _____

10. Put a charge on your balloon with another 20 rubbings. Try picking up the seeds, grass, leaves, and other smaller particles listed on the previous page in the materials section. How close do you have to be to attract some of the heavier pieces?

    _____

    Try chalk dust, lint, and any other light pieces you can find. Describe your results.

    _____

    _____

11. Which materials were the easiest to pick up with the balloon?

    _____

    _____

12. Were you unable to pick up some of the materials? Were they too heavy?

    _____

    _____

13. How long did it take for the seeds, grass, leaves, and other material to fall off the balloon?

    _____

    _____

STATIC PICK-UPS

JOURNAL ENTRY

1. What was the easiest material to pick up? What type of rubbing provided the best static charge?

_____

_____

_____

2. How could you make a game out of these static-electricity experiences?

_____

_____

_____

3. How could you help someone take lint off a piece of clothing with a balloon?

_____

_____

_____

4. Which activity did you enjoy the most in these static-electricity tests? Why?

_____

_____

_____

5. What did you learn from these static-electricity experiences?

_____

_____

_____

DESIGN PROCESS REVIEW—STATIC PICK-UPS

Share your journal entries and experiences with your class during a discussion moderated by your teacher.

Ⓝ Ⓐ Ⓜ Ⓔ _____

IT'S ELECTRIFYING!

CHALLENGE ACTIVITY—ATTRACTED OR REPULSED?

You have been working with static electricity for three periods now and experiencing it since your parents first combed your hair as a very young child. (Young children often have light, thin, hair that provides an excellent static charge on a comb.) You may design and develop your own experiment based on your previous experiences or use one of the choices below as a starting point. Use the Design Process Worksheet on page 5 to help you.

CHOICES TO CONSIDER

1. Plan and conduct an experiment to determine which student's hair or article of clothing creates the best static charge.

2. Make static streamers. Cut thin strips of notebook or plain white paper about 3 inches long. Place a static charge on a balloon or comb. Hold the charged item next to the long, thin strips. Can you see a static reaction? Try using tissue paper or thin strips of aluminum foil cut in the same way.

3. Become an Electric Student. Decorate your clothes, hair, face, arms, or legs with static-producing material or several balloons. The other team member will try to create the best charge or the most dramatic static response for hair or other materials.

or

TAKE THE CHALLENGE! ATTRACTED OR REPULSED?

(This activity requires participation from multiple class members.)

Each student should use their own balloon. Tie a piece of fishing line about 6 inches long on the knotted end of the balloon. Place a good static charge on the balloon. Rub it on your hair—*one way only*—10 to 20 times.

While holding your balloon by the fishing line, check each student to see if it is pushed away—repulsed—by the other person's balloon or attracted to it. (You can also see if the other person's hair or clothes are attracted to or repulsed by the balloon.) You may need to "recharge" your balloon throughout the activity.

Record your results on the next page.

IT'S ELECTRIFYING!

CHALLENGE ACTIVITY—CHARTING RESULTS

Use a computer to make a table like the one below.

1. Open **Word** or **Google Docs**.
2. Click on the **Table** and insert a table. You will need to fill in how many rows and columns you need.

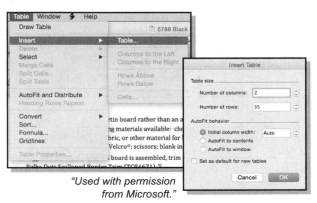

"Used with permission from Microsoft."

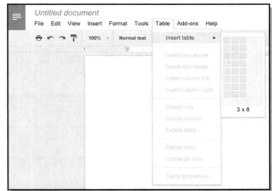

©2015 Google Inc, used with permission. Google and the Google logo are registered trademarks of Google Inc.

3. The table should have 2 columns and as many rows as there are students in your class.
4. Your empty table will appear on your page.
5. You can make adjustments by going back to **Table** on the menu bar. You can make the size of the cells different, and you can add or delete rows and columns.
6. Label the table and fill it in with the results of testing your balloon. Add any notes and observations that you made while testing.

NAME	ATTRACTED (YES/NO)
1.	
2.	
3.	
4.	
5.	
6.	
7.	
8.	
9.	
10.	
11.	
12.	
13.	
14.	

NAME _____

IT'S ELECTRIFYING!

CHALLENGE ACTIVITY—ENGINEERING PROCESS

Use the lines below to describe each step of your process during this challenge activity.

1. **Learning Objective** (What do you wish to discover?)

   _____

   _____

2. **Procedure** (What you plan to do, build, make, or produce in the experiment? Be specific.)

   _____

   _____

   _____

   _____

3. **Materials Needed** (Choose available materials from the classroom.)

   _____

   _____

4. **Problems** (What difficulties did you encounter?)

   _____

   _____

   _____

5. **Results** (What happened?)

   _____

   _____

   _____

   _____

6. **What did you learn?**

   _____

   _____

   _____

IT'S ELECTRIFYING!

CHALLENGE ACTIVITY—JOURNAL ENTRY

Use a computer, tablet, or other device to answer each paragraph subject below. Be sure to use paragraph format and complete sentences.

PARAGRAPH 1

Which experiment in the unit impressed you the most? Why? What was new to you in some way?

PARAGRAPH 2

What did you learn about static electricity—either during today's activity or the entire unit?

PARAGRAPH 3

What use do you think you could find for static electricity? Explain your answer. Be creative!

PARAGRAPH 4

What is the difference between static electricity and current electricity flowing into your home or school? Which is more useful? Which is more interesting?

PARAGRAPH 5

Which experiment with static electricity would you like to do again? Why?

PARAGRAPH 6

Respond to these questions by referring back to the activities you completed in this unit.

1. *How does static electricity occur in everyday life?*
2. *How can static electricity be created or used in the classroom?*
3. *What materials are very effective in creating static charges?*
4. *When have you encountered static charges?*
5. *Why can't you plug into a source of static electricity?*

DESIGN PROCESS REVIEW—STATIC ELECTRICITY

Share your journal entries, experiences, observations, and questions with your classmates in the class discussion your teacher leads to culminate the unit.

STRUCTURES

4 Sessions: 1 session per each activity (approximately 1 to $1\frac{1}{2}$ hours per session)

CONNECTIONS AND SUGGESTIONS

SCIENCE—Students will be constructing model housing structures and multiple units using playing cards to model the shapes and forms of larger structures. They need to be concerned with maximizing their space and using the available materials to create structures that are durable. They will have limited amounts of material, as do real construction engineers. They will need to use reinforcements to protect against wind and earthquake damage. They will use a limited amount of reinforcements materials for aesthetic (and cost) reasons.

TECHNOLOGY—For this project, students can use basic computer software to write a brief report in which they describe the problems encountered, the solutions attempted, the success rate of each activity, the different approaches used, and any suggestions for improvement. The final journal entry can also be used for students to evaluate the project.

ENGINEERING—Students will experiment with a variety of engineering designs and the listed materials to create model housing structures. Emphasis will be on working with limited space and material while maximizing security against wind and earthquakes.

MATH—Students will use their understanding of area, perimeter, and volume to record the use of available space and to measure the features of their structures.

Materials

- decks of playing cards (one for each pair of students) or sturdy 3" × 5" index cards cut in half
- rulers
- small electric fan/hand-held fan/hair dryer
- masking tape, small sticky notes, or round stickers
- modeling clay (1 stick per team—approximately 1 ounce)
- scissors

· UNIT 4 VOCABULARY ·

architect—a building designer

area—the number of unit squares in a flat shape—often measured in square inches or square feet

bungalow—a small, one-story house

condominium—one unit in a multiple-unit dwelling

durable—tough, long-lasting

engineer—an individual who plans, builds, and/or maintains machines or structures

evaluate—to make a judgment

exterior—the outside of a building

horizontal—flat, even with the earth

interior—the inside of a building

intersection—a place where two walls meet

reinforce—to support or strengthen

retrofit—to modify, adapt, or upgrade something that has already been built

vertical—straight up and down

volume—the amount of space in a figure, calculated using the length, width, and height

DISCUSSION PROMPT:

Many cities and countries that have occurrences of earthquakes are required to retrofit their old buildings to make them earthquake-safe. Often, though, the cost of retrofitting is more expensive than the buildings themselves. Also, many areas don't have the money to bring buildings up to modern standards—and neither do the owners or residents of the buildings. Therefore, many times people will suggest that a building be demolished in order to rebuild it as earthquake-safe in a less costly manner. What if this was a dilemma you faced for your own house? How would you decide to make your home safer?

BUILDING STRUCTURES

A structure is an arrangement of parts that form a system that is capable of supporting loads. A building is a man-made structure with a roof and walls, standing more or less permanently in one place—such as a house or factory. Buildings come in all shapes and sizes and serve several needs of society. They can be used as shelter from weather, for security, as a living space, to provide privacy, to store belongings, and to work in. Structures in one part of the world may look very different from structures in a different part of the world. Structures near a large body of water, such as the Amazon River, are often built on stilts in order to protect these structures from floods and to protect the inhabitants from wild animals. In very hot climates, such as the Sahara Desert in Africa, structures are often built underground in order to protect people from the harsh temperatures. Some structures, such as yurts, are built with materials that are easy to take down and carry, so that the people living in them can move easily from place to place. Some structures are carved out of caves, some are made of snow and ice, and some are even built in trees.

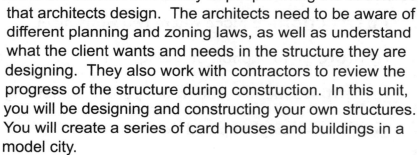

Architecture is a general term to describe buildings and other physical structures. Architects are people who plan, design, and/or oversee the construction of buildings and other structures. The architects decisions affect the comfort and safety of people using the structures that architects design. The architects need to be aware of different planning and zoning laws, as well as understand what the client wants and needs in the structure they are designing. They also work with contractors to review the progress of the structure during construction. In this unit, you will be designing and constructing your own structures. You will create a series of card houses and buildings in a model city.

Use a computer or tablet to search for information on the Internet to help you as you complete the activities in this unit. Helpful search terms include:

architecture   home design   structure

earthquake-resistant structures   seismic retrofit

SIMPLE STRUCTURES

Directions: Work in teams of two as you perform this first activity. Gather these materials as instructed by your teacher.

> ## TEAM MATERIALS
> - electric fan or hair dryer
> - masking tape, small sticky notes, or round stickers
> - modeling clay (1 stick per team—approximately 1 ounce)
>
> - playing cards (1 deck of 52 cards per team) or sturdy 3" × 5" index cards cut in half
> - rulers
> - scissors

GETTING STARTED

You and your partner will use a deck of 52 playing cards (or 3" × 5" index cards cut in half) to construct card houses that will remain standing in the face of wind (from an electric fan or hair dryer) and an earthquake (from shaking the desk). You will use very small portions of modeling clay and a limited number of stickers, sticky notes, or small pieces of tape for connecting the cards and keeping them upright.

With scissors, cut your one ounce of clay into about 20 to 25 pea-sized balls.

TESTING MATERIALS

Carefully use six cards to build a simple card house with four sides and a roof. The cards should be horizontal for the walls, and two of the cards should be used on top for the roof. Do NOT use any clay or stickers to hold your cards together.

Stand about 3 feet away from the structures. Use a small electric (or hand-held) fan to create a wind to test the durability of the structure. (Most likely, your structure will fall. Don't worry! This is part of the engineering process!)

STARTING OVER—WORKING WITH REINFORCEMENT AND ARRANGEMENT

1. Rebuild the walls of the house. This time, use one pea-sized piece of modeling clay to anchor each of the walls at each corner. Use a very small amount of clay, the size of a pea or a kernel of corn, at the base where the walls intersect.

2. Use 2 cards to create the roof. They may overlap somewhat. Attach the cards with stickers (or sticky notes). You may want to use one sticky note at each upper corner of the house.

SIMPLE STRUCTURES

TESTING FOR WIND RESISTANCE

1. Use a fan on the lowest setting to test the durability of this house. Position the fan near and then above the structure. (Try 3 feet away and then 2 feet away.)

   Did the structure remain standing? _____

   _____

   Did the roof remain intact? _____

   _____

2. Repair your house, if needed. Use a small electric fan or hair dryer located about 5 feet from the house on the lowest setting. Then, increase the setting to a moderate speed and then to the highest setting. Aim the fan above the house and then lower it until it gives the house direct force at about 5 feet away.

   What damage did the wind do?

   _____

   _____

   _____

3. What setting did the most damage? Did the house survive the wind at the lowest and moderate setting? Explain your answer.

   _____

   _____

   _____

4. How could you have prevented some of the damage? What could you have put on the roof or the corners of the roof in order to prevent damage?

   _____

   _____

   _____

SIMPLE STRUCTURES

TESTING FOR EARTHQUAKE RESISTANCE

Test your card structure's resistance to earthquakes by creating your own earthquake.

1. **Level One—Light Shaking or Trembler**

   Shake the desk gently with a light push two or three times. Record what happened to the structure. Repair the structure, if needed.

   _____

   _____

   _____

   _____

2. **Level Two—One Good Jolt with Small Aftershocks**

   Shake the desk sharply once and follow with two or three light shakes. Record what happened to the structure. Repair the structure, if needed.

   _____

   _____

   _____

   _____

3. **Level Three—Several Sharp Jolts with Aftershocks**

   Shake the desk sharply at least three times and follow with three or four light movements. Record what happened to the structure.

   _____

   _____

   _____

   _____

 NAME _____

SIMPLE STRUCTURES

RETROFITTING YOUR STRUCTURE

Create a different style of card house, this time with two rooms, using 10 cards. Reuse or rebuild the four walls of your original structure. Add three more walls on one end of the structure to create a two-room house. The one pea-sized lump of clay will hold three walls in the interior of your house on each of the two middle intersections. Others can still be used on corners with only two walls. You can arrange your roof as you did with one room, or try to fit three cards to form a roof over the two rooms. To keep the roof secure, you can use tape, a sticker, or a sticky note connecting each of the cards.

Remember: Consider these questions:

1. Would a small pea-sized ball of clay help hold the roof on?
2. Would one or two extra pieces of clay provide enough support for the walls to hold during a moderate wind (from the fan) or earthquake (from you and your partner)?

Field-test your two-room house with your fan and manufactured earthquake.

Sketch your house in the boxes below before and after testing.

BEFORE WIND/EARTHQUAKE	AFTER WIND/EARTHQUAKE

SIMPLE STRUCTURES

JOURNAL ENTRY

1. How well did your structure survive the wind created by your fan? Did the structure survive the mild winds, moderate winds, or even the strong ones?

   _____

   _____

   _____

   _____

2. After you repaired what was needed, how did your new structure survive the earthquakes you produced? Did it resist the mild shaking? Did some or all of the structure survive the strong quakes you produced?

   _____

   _____

   _____

   _____

3. What minor changes could you make to strengthen your new structure with the materials you have?

   _____

   _____

   _____

   _____

4. Is there another shape you could use to modify the structure and try to make it stronger?

   _____

   _____

   _____

   _____

DESIGN PROCESS REVIEW—SIMPLE STRUCTURES

Share your journal entries and building experiences with your classmates during a discussion led by your teacher. Look (and ask!) for ideas to improve your structure.

 **NAME** _____

MULTI-ROOM STRUCTURES

Directions: Work in teams of two as you perform this activity. Gather these materials as directed by your teacher.

> ### TEAM MATERIALS
> - 10–15 small squares of masking tape, small sticky notes, or round stickers
> - electric fan or hair dryer
> - modeling clay (about 1 ounce per team)
> - playing cards (one deck of cards per team) or sturdy 3" × 5" index cards cut in half
> - rulers

BUILDING MULTIPLE-ROOM HOMES—FOUR-ROOM BUNGALOW

In the last unit, you built a two-room house. In this activity, you will create multi-room houses using the same materials as you used in the last activity.

Start by expanding your structure to a four-room bungalow like the one shown to the right.

Arrange cards to form a room that is two cards long and two cards wide. You will use a total of eight cards for the outside of the house, arranged the long way on their sides. Use four more cards for room dividers. Use small balls of clay to support the cards at the base and tape, sticky notes, or stickers to connect them by the sides. Use four cards for the roof.

THINKING BEYOND THE BOX

One of the strongest shapes is the triangle. Build another structure using your cards and clay, but use the triangle arrangement shown to the right as a start.

Lay your cards upright the long way, as before. Use your balls of clay at each corner. Use one piece of tape at the top of each corner to help hold the sides together and hold the roof when you lay the cards for that feature.

Place two more cards upright the long way next to the triangle, making two triangular rooms as shown. Use the balls of clay already in place—and the tape—to create this reinforced building.

MULTI-ROOM STRUCTURES

TESTING THE BUNGALOW AND TRIANGULAR STRUCTURES

Test each structure as you did in the previous activity. Turn on a fan at its lowest speed and then speed it up with each trial. (Start by placing the fan 5 feet away and then move closer.)

WIND TEST

What were your results with the bungalow?

Fan at Low Speed: _____

_____

Fan at High Speed: _____

_____

What were your results with the triangular structure?

Fan at Low Speed: _____

_____

Fan at High Speed: _____

_____

EARTHQUAKE TEST

Rebuild your structures (if needed) and test them with your earthquake procedures. Record the results.

Bungalow Results

1. Level One—Light Shaking or Trembler

   _____

   _____

2. Level Two—One Good Jolt with Small Aftershocks

   _____

   _____

3. Level Three—Several Sharp Jolts with Aftershocks

   _____

   _____

Triangle Results

Level One—Light Shaking or Trembler

   _____

   _____

Level Two—One Good Jolt with Small Aftershocks

   _____

   _____

Level Three—Several Sharp Jolts with Aftershocks

   _____

   _____

MULTI-ROOM STRUCTURES

MATH MATTERS

It is important to know the exact size of any engineering project you might work on. Many prices for goods, services, or the purchase of these construction projects are based on the square footage of the buildings, the amount of land they cover, and the cost of the materials needed. Architects and engineers have to be very concerned about how much material, of any kind, is used and how much total land area is involved. They are also concerned with issues related to size for legal and safety reasons.

You are going to compute the area, perimeters, and volumes of some of your structures. Use your calculator or computer to help you do the math computations, if needed.

Measure the length of one card and record it here in centimeters: _____ cm

Measure the width of one card and record it here in centimeters: _____ cm

Perimeter (distance around a structure—add all sides)

Each side of your bungalow is two cards long. How long is one side? _____ cm

How long is the perimeter of your bungalow (all four sides)? _____ cm

Area (Floor space—length × width)

What is the length of your bungalow multiplied by the width of your bungalow? _____ cm^2

Volume (amount of space in entire bungalow—length × width × height)

What is the length of your bungalow multiplied by the width of your bungalow multiplied by the height (width of card) of your bungalow? _____ cm^3

 NAME _____

MULTI-ROOM STRUCTURES

JOURNAL ENTRY

1. How do you think a two- or three-story house would survive your disaster tests?

   _____

   _____

   _____

2. What could you do to create a more durable multi-room building?

   _____

   _____

   _____

3. What house shape would be most effective? Why?

   _____

   _____

   _____

4. How would you compute the amount of air in a room 10 cm long, 10 cm wide, and 10 cm high? What is the answer?

   _____

   _____

   _____

5. How would you compute the size of the floor in a structure 20 cm long and 10 cm wide? What is the answer?

   _____

   _____

   _____

DESIGN PROCESS REVIEW—MULTI-ROOM STRUCTURES

Share your journal entries and building experiences with your classmates during a discussion led by your teacher. Look (and ask!) for ideas to improve your structure.

 NAME _____

MULTI-LEVEL STRUCTURES

Directions: Work in teams of two as you perform this activity. Gather these materials as directed by your teacher.

> ### TEAM MATERIALS
> - 10–15 small squares of masking tape, small sticky notes, or round stickers
> - electric fan or hair dryer
> - modeling clay (about 1 ounce per team)
> - playing cards (one deck of cards per team) or sturdy 3" × 5" index cards cut in half
> - rulers

CREATING TWO-STORY STRUCTURES

1. Use your cards to create either the triangular structure or the traditional four-sided, two-room structure you started with in the first activity. Remember to be sparing in your use of balls of clay and tape.

2. Attach a second room to the side of whichever structure you chose to work with.

3. Create a third structure to place on top of one of the rooms. Be careful to position this structure exactly on top of only one lower-level structure.

4. Build a fourth structure to place on top of the remaining part of the lower structure. You now have a four-room, two-story apartment.

   Sketch your structure in the box below.

MULTI-LEVEL STRUCTURES

TESTING THE STRUCTURES

Test your structure as you did in the previous activity. Turn on a fan at its lowest speed and then speed it up with each trial. (Start by placing the fan 5 feet away and then move closer.)

What were your results with the two-story structure?

WIND TEST

Fan at Low Speed: _____

_____

Fan at High Speed: _____

_____

EARTHQUAKE TEST

Rebuild your structure (if needed) and test them with your earthquake procedures. Record the results.

1. Level One—Light Shaking or Trembler

   _____

   _____

   _____

2. Level Two—One Good Jolt with Small Aftershocks

   _____

   _____

   _____

3. Level Three—Several Sharp Jolts with Aftershocks

   _____

   _____

   _____

 N A M E _____

MULTI-LEVEL STRUCTURES

THREE-STORY STRUCTURE

Now, add a third level to your structure by adding two more apartments to create a six-room, three-story building. Remember to use balls of clay and tape to attach the levels. Test the structure in the same manner as before.

What were your results?

WIND TEST

Fan at Low Speed: _____

_____

Fan at High Speed: _____

_____

EARTHQUAKE TEST

Rebuild your structure (if needed) and test them with your earthquake procedures. Record the results.

1. Level One—Light Shaking or Trembler

   _____

   _____

   _____

2. Level Two—One Good Jolt with Small Aftershocks

   _____

   _____

   _____

3. Level Three—Several Sharp Jolts with Aftershocks

   _____

   _____

   _____

MULTI-LEVEL STRUCTURES

DO THE MATH

Compute the area, perimeter, and volume of the two-story structure you created. Use the same formulas from the calculations of the four-room bungalow.

Perimeter of the two-story structure

Length of structure: _____ cm

Width of structure: _____ cm

Total perimeter: _____ cm

Area (length × width) of the two-story structure

Length of structure: _____ cm   Width of structure: _____ cm   Total Area: _____ cm²

Volume (length × width × height) of the two-story structure

Length of structure: _____ cm   Height of structure: _____ cm

Width of structure: _____ cm   Total volume: _____ cm³

Now compute the area, perimeter, and volume of the three-story structure you created.

Perimeter of the three-story structure

Length of structure: _____ cm

Width of structure: _____ cm

Total perimeter: _____ cm

Area (length × width) of the three-story structure

Length of structure: _____ cm   Width of structure: _____ cm   Total Area: _____ cm²

Volume (length × width × height) of the three-story structure

Length of structure: _____ cm   Height of structure: _____ cm

Width of structure: _____ cm   Total volume: _____ cm³

Compare the answers for the two-story and three-story structures. What do you notice?

_____

_____

_____

_____

 _____

MULTI-LEVEL STRUCTURES

JOURNAL ENTRY

1. Which structure worked best for you—the triangular design or the square design? Explain why you chose the design you did.

   _____

   _____

   _____

   _____

2. What have you learned about making taller structures? What should you avoid? What should you be sure to do?

   _____

   _____

   _____

   _____

3. How could you calculate the volume of a two-story building if the second story was a different size than the first?

   _____

   _____

   _____

   _____

4. How could you reinforce your structure at higher levels? How could paper clips help stabilize the structure?

   _____

   _____

   _____

   _____

DESIGN PROCESS REVIEW—MULTI-LEVEL STRUCTURES

Share your journal entries and building experiences with your classmates during a discussion led by your teacher. Ask for ideas to improve your structure.

CONSTRUCTION ZONE: MULTI-LEVEL STRUCTURES

CHALLENGE ACTIVITY—CREATE YOUR OWN MULTI-LEVEL STRUCTURES

These pages are designed to stimulate your imagination with some suggestions for the project. You will probably want to work with one or two other teams to combine your work and display it. Use the Design Process Worksheet on page 5 to help guide your work.

TEAM MATERIALS
- electric fan or hair dryer
- masking tape or small sticky notes
- modeling clay
- paper clips
- playing cards or index cards
- rulers

- Gather your notes from the previous exercises in this unit. Compare each structure made for durability, strength, and attractiveness.

- Build extra structures ahead of time, or as needed, when you start building high.

- For all structures, especially these higher buildings, check that the balls of clay are connected to all adjacent cards.

TRY THIS—CHOICES TO CONSIDER

THE SIX-PLEX

1. Start by assembling a six-plex apartment arrangement with three units on the bottom floor in a line. Make sure the tape/sticky notes and balls of clay are firmly attached.

2. Place the next two units centered on top of the three as shown to the right. Use tape/sticky notes and/or balls of clay to attach the two structures to the three below.

3. Place the final unit centered on top of the two mid-level units.

ARRANGING AN APARTMENT COMPLEX— CONSTRUCTION TEAM (FOUR TO EIGHT WORKERS)

You can use the staggered approach described above to assemble more structures in the same style. You can also build a series of ground-floor units. Center a second layer of units on three base units as you did with the six-plex. Assemble the third story on top of the second layer by staggering these structures as well. Use your tape/sticky notes and balls of clay to securely attach these units.

_____

CONSTRUCTION ZONE: MULTI-LEVEL STRUCTURES

CHALLENGE ACTIVITY—CREATE YOUR OWN MULTI-LEVEL STRUCTURES

BUILD A TOWER

Build a tower (at least nine levels!) according to your own design. Use a staggered system as suggested on the previous page or try to build straight up three levels, stagger the next layer, build straight up on this staggered layer two more layers, and stagger again and build three more layers. (You would have nine layers with each set of three layers forming a smaller block as the tower gets taller.)

What type of structure are you going to build?

_____

How many levels will it have?

_____

How many rooms/apartments will each level have? (List each level separately.)

_____

_____

How are you going to make sure the levels are all solidly constructed?

_____

_____

Sketch your structure in the box below.

 NAME _____

CONSTRUCTION ZONE: MULTI-LEVEL STRUCTURES

CHALLENGE ACTIVITY—CREATE YOUR OWN MULTI-LEVEL STRUCTURES

TEST YOUR STRUCTURE

Before you run the tests, check to see that all structures are securely fit together with balls of clay and tape/sticky notes.

Test each structure as you did in the previous activity. Turn on a fan at its lowest speed and then speed it up with each trial. (You can also increase wind intensity by placing the fan 5 feet away and then move closer.)

Record Your Results

Wind Test

Fan at Low Speed: _____

_____

Fan at High Speed: _____

_____

Earthquake Test

Rebuild your structures (if needed) and test them with your earthquake procedures. Record the results.

1. Level One—Light Shaking or Trembler

   _____

   _____

2. Level Two—One Good Jolt with Small Aftershocks

   _____

   _____

3. Level Three—Several Sharp Jolts with Aftershocks

   _____

   _____

_____

CONSTRUCTION ZONE: MULTI-LEVEL STRUCTURES

CHALLENGE ACTIVITY—JOURNAL ENTRY

Use a computer, tablet, or other device to answer each paragraph subject below. Be sure to use paragraph format and complete sentences.

PARAGRAPH 1

Describe how you built and arranged your most successful structure.

PARAGRAPH 2

What techniques for reinforcing structures did you learn that you might find useful in building any structure?

PARAGRAPH 3

What special problems did you encounter in building your higher structures and keeping them stable?

PARAGRAPH 4

Would you like to become a construction engineer or architect? Explain your response.

PARAGRAPH 5

Why do you think engineers and architects build models of their projects as you did (but with more details)?

PARAGRAPH 6

Respond to these questions by referring back to the activities you completed in this unit.

1. *What is the best design for using every bit of available space in an area?*
2. *How high can you build a playing-card structure?*
3. *How strong of a wind will a well-made card structure survive?*
4. *How strong of an earthquake will a carefully-built card structure survive?*
5. *What techniques can you use to build a taller, stronger structure?*

DESIGN PROCESS REVIEW—CONSTRUCTION ZONE: MULTI-LEVEL STRUCTURES

Share your structures and construction experiences with your classmates in the class discussion/presentations your teacher leads to culminate this unit.

KITCHEN CHEMISTRY

> **5 Sessions:** 1 session per each activity (approximately 1 to $1\frac{1}{2}$ hours per session)

CONNECTIONS AND SUGGESTIONS

SCIENCE—In these experiments, students will combine an acid (vinegar) with a base (baking soda) to produce a controlled explosion that launches a cork rocket with the carbon dioxide gas produced. They will also discover the cleansing properties of an acid (vinegar) in cleaning coins. Students will create carbon dioxide in a glass of water. The carbon dioxide bubbles act as mini floats for the popcorn seeds. They will also soak bones in vinegar to leach out the calcium—making bones somewhat rubbery. They will observe the changing of materials through chemical action, and the use of new substances, and they will discover uses for common chemicals.

TECHNOLOGY—The apparatuses created for these activities represent some of the technological applications. For these projects, students will also use basic computer software to write a brief report in which they describe the problems encountered, the solutions attempted, the success rate of each activity, the different approaches used, and any suggestions for improvement. The final journal entry can also be used for students to evaluate the project.

ENGINEERING—The engineering applications require a very specific use of materials and measuring tools, and they emphasize the need for using tools and adding materials in a specific order. Students will work with elements of design to use chemicals to create a small rocket, to clean pennies, and to change the compositions of eggshell and bone.

MATH—Math applications involve measuring chemicals, computing percentages, ratios, fractions, determining distances, and comparing dates on coins. Mode, median, mean, and range are calculated and used.

Materials

- 1-ounce (30 cc) measuring cups
- baking soda
- chalk
- clear plastic cups (8 oz.)
- eggs or eggshells
- empty plastic water bottles
- eyedroppers
- facial tissue
- fishing line
- food coloring
- light seeds (any kind)
- magnifying glasses
- masking tape
- paper or plastic-coated plates
- paper towels
- pennies and other coins (old, not shiny)
- plastic teaspoons
- popping corn
- small cups (1 oz. and 6 oz.)
- small rocks and gravel (from a variety of sources)
- straws
- turkey or chicken bones
- watch/stopwatch
- water
- white vinegar
- wine corks
- yardsticks or metersticks

— UNIT 5 VOCABULARY —

compounds—chemical combinations of two or more elements

diffusion—the spreading out of molecules within a solution

elements—chemical substances consisting of atoms that cannot be separated into simpler substances

median—the middle number in a group of numbers arranged from smallest to largest

mean—the number equal to the sum of a set of numbers divided by how many numbers are in the set

mode—the most frequently-occuring number in a set of numbers

pH—a numeric scale used to specify the acidity or alkalinity of a solution

propellant—a chemical substance used in the production of energy in order to create movement of an object

range—the difference between the largest and smallest numbers in a set of numbers

ratio—the relationship in quantity, amount, or size between two or more things

reaction—a chemical change

DISCUSSION PROMPT:

In this unit you will be experimenting with different chemicals and how they interact with other substances. One of the experiments is putting an egg in vinegar (an acid). Often this experiment is done to show the effects of acid and other harsh ingredients on teeth. Soda is acidic, and it can weaken enamel on teeth as well as stain them. Can you think of some other foods or drinks that you know are bad for your teeth? What do you think will happen to the egg when it is put in vinegar?

KITCHEN CHEMISTRY

Chemistry is the science that is concerned with the composition of materials and how they can be changed by chemical action. Everything in the universe, from a giant skyscraper to a tiny ant, is made of atoms that combine with other atoms to create molecules. These molecules are also very small. There are said to be more than a septillion (1,000,000,000,000,000,000,000,000) molecules in a single drop of water (1.7 septillion to be exact).

Atoms combine with each other in a process called chemical bonding. The negatively charged electrons that are orbiting the nucleus and the positively charged protons in the nucleus are attracted to each other. A chemical bond allows the formation of chemical substances that have two or more atoms. For example, two hydrogen (H) atoms bond with an oxygen (O) atom to create a water molecule, written as H_2O. A sodium (Na) atom combines with a chloride (Cl) atom to create sodium chloride (NaCl), or common table salt. In chemical bonds, the atoms combine but remain unchanged in that they contain the same physical substances as when they were individual atoms.

A chemical reaction occurs when substances are combined and there is a chemical change in the substances. One chemical reaction you might be familiar with is the mixing of baking soda and vinegar. Vinegar, an acid, reacts with baking soda, a base, and the reaction forms water and carbon dioxide, a gas (the bubbles you see in the reaction). You will be using this chemical reaction in an activity to fuel rockets!

Use a computer or tablet to search for information on the Internet to help you as you complete the activities in this unit. Helpful search terms include:

acid	bonds	molecules	oxidize
atoms	compounds	neutrons	particles
base	electrons	nucleus	protons

 NAME _____

WORKING WITH ACID

Directions: Work in teams of two as you perform this first activity. Gather these materials as directed by your teacher.

TEAM MATERIALS

- chalk
- clear plastic cups
- dried chicken or turkey bones
- eggshells and/or eggs

- eyedroppers
- magnifying glasses
- paper or plastic-coated plates

- small rocks and gravel from a variety of sources
- white vinegar

CAUTION: When handling vinegar or any other acid, keep hands away from faces and eyes, and wash your hands when you are done.

EGGSHELL INVESTIGATION

1. Place a full or partial eggshell or a whole egg into a clear plastic cup. Pour about 3 ounces of vinegar into the cup so the eggshell is covered.
2. Use the magnifying glass to carefully examine the surface of the eggshell. Look for bubbles on the surface of the shell.
3. How do the bubbles form on the shell? Are the bubbles large, small, or various sizes?

_____

_____

_____

4. Write your names on the cup and leave it in a protected place where you can observe it regularly during the class period. After an agreed-upon time designated by your teacher, check your eggshell again.

   a. How many bubbles do you now have on your eggshell? _____

   b. Are there more or less bubbles than you had before? _____

   c. Do some of the bubbles pop off, or do they stay on the shell? _____

   d. What is happening to the shell itself? _____

   _____

   e. What do you think will happen to the shell by tomorrow? Why? _____

   _____

5. Check the egg after a few days to see what changes have occurred. Record the changes here.

   _____

   _____

   _____

   Draw a sketch in the box of your egg/eggshell after a couple of days have passed.

NAME _____

WORKING WITH ACID

TESTING FOR CALCITE

Calcite is a common mineral found in many rocks. It will bubble when exposed to a mild acid such as vinegar.

1. Spread several small gravel-sized pieces of rock on a paper or plastic-coated plate.
2. Use the eyedropper to pick up a small amount of vinegar.
3. Place one or two drops on a piece of gravel or a few drops on a larger rock.
4. Use a magnifying glass to examine each area where you put the vinegar. Look for very small bubbles on the surface of the rock or gravel. Do not necessarily expect to find bubbles everywhere. Calcite is often mixed with many other minerals in rocks. The bubbles you find will indicate where the calcite is.
5. Describe your results.

    a. How many bubbles have formed on the gravel and rocks? _____

    _____

    b. Are you able to determine which rocks have calcite? _____

    _____

    c. Where have you seen rocks and gravel that resemble your specimens? _____

    _____

    Draw a sketch of what you observed in the box below.

6. Now place a small piece of chalk on the plate. Put a few drops of vinegar on the chalk and describe what happens.

_____

_____

 NAME

WORKING WITH ACID

MAKING RUBBER BONES

1. Take your chicken or turkey bone (or other small bone) and place it in a clear plastic cup with vinegar. Make sure there is enough vinegar to cover the bone.
2. Observe the bone. Look for bubbles (as you did with the eggshell). They will take longer to form on the bone. Write your names on the cup and let the bone sit in the vinegar for a few class periods (or a couple of days).

INVESTIGATION RESULTS

After a few days of letting the bone sit in the vinegar, observe it a final time and answer the questions below.

1. How many bubbles can you count on the bone?

_____

_____

2. Are there areas on the bone with few bubbles and others with many bubbles?

_____

_____

3. Gently bend the bone. Is it more flexible than it was when you started? Has the bone changed? How?

_____

_____

4. What do you think this investigation shows about how the bones in your body would react to an acid?

_____

_____

5. List some acids that you know are safe to eat or drink or are found in foods or beverages.

_____

_____

 NAME _____

WORKING WITH ACID

JOURNAL ENTRY

1. Which was the most interesting investigation you did in Activity 1? Why?

   _____

   _____

   _____

   _____

2. Think about the information you discovered. How might you use it in your personal life?

   _____

   _____

   _____

   _____

3. Did you learn anything that you could teach a parent or another family member? Explain.

   _____

   _____

   _____

   _____

4. What other experiments could you do with vinegar?

   _____

   _____

   _____

   _____

DESIGN PROCESS REVIEW—WORKING WITH ACID

Share your journal entries and observations with your classmates during a discussion led by your teacher.

NAME _____

CLEANING PENNIES

Directions: Work in teams of two as you perform this activity. Gather these materials as directed by your teacher.

TEAM MATERIALS
- eyedroppers
- magnifying glasses
- old pennies (not shiny)
- paper or plastic-coated plates
- vinegar
- water
- watch/stopwatch

CAUTION: When handling vinegar or any other acid, keep hands away from faces and eyes, and wash your hands when you are done.

GETTING STARTED

1. Place five pennies on your paper plate. Fill an eyedropper with vinegar and squeeze two or three drops of vinegar onto each penny head.

2. Time how long it takes the pennies to be noticeably brighter: _____

3. Use the method above to clean 20 pennies. Create a chart (using the instructions below) to record the amount of time it takes for them to become brighter. Record the year on the penny in your chart. One partner should add a drop of vinegar to the penny while the other partner starts the stopwatch. Stop the watch when the penny has transformed, and then record the time. Repeat for each penny.

CHARTING RESULTS

Use a computer to make a table like the one below.

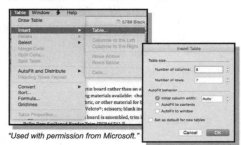

"Used with permission from Microsoft."

1. Open **Word** or **Google Docs**.

2. Click on **Table** and insert a table. The table should have 8 columns and 7 rows.

4. Your empty table will appear on your page.

5. You can make adjustments by going back to **Table** on the menu bar. You can make the size of the cells different and you can add or delete rows and columns.

6. Label the table and fill it in with the results of cleaning your pennies. Add any notes and observations that you made while testing.

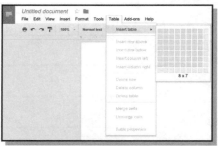

©2015 Google Inc, used with permission. Google and the Google logo are registered trademarks of Google Inc.

CLEANING TIME AND YEARS FOR 20 PENNIES							
CLEAN TIME	YEAR	CLEAN TIME	YEAR	CLEAN TIME	YEAR	CLEAN TIME	YEAR

CLEANING PENNIES

PENNY MATH—MODE, MEAN, MEDIAN, AND RANGE

1. The **mode** is a math term for the most frequently occurring number in a group of numbers. Which year is the mode for your 20 pennies? (If there are no repeated years, there is no mode. If two years are repeated the same amount of times, there is a double mode and both are recorded.)

   Penny modes: _____

2. The **mean** is the average of all 20 years. Add them together. Divide the total by the number of years (20). (You may use a calculator if your teacher approves.)

   List the years to add: _____

   _____

   _____

   Total of all 20 years added together: _____

   Divide the total by 20 (the number of years added together). Mean: _____

3. The **range** is the difference between the smallest number and the largest number (year).

   _____ – _____ = _____
   largest (latest) year   the smallest (earliest) year

4. The **median** is the middle number in a group of numbers that is ordered from least to greatest.

   a. Put the years in order from earliest to most recent. _____

   _____

   b. If the two middle years—the 10th and the 11th—are the same, that is the median.

   c. If the two middle years are different, add them together and divide by 2 (even if you get a fraction). Add the two middle years—the 10th and 11th. Divide the number by 2.

   Add the two middle years: _____ + _____ = _____

   Divide the total by 2. The median = _____

5. Wash 15 of your pennies in tap water. Leave 5 pennies overnight on the plate or until the next period. When you examine the pennies, look for signs of corrosion, wear, or damage caused by the mild acid, vinegar. Describe any changes on the lines below.

   _____

   _____

   _____

 **NAME** _____

CLEANING PENNIES

JOURNAL ENTRY

1. Did the pennies look new or were they merely clean? Explain your answer.

   _____

   _____

   _____

   _____

2. Would soap and water have made the pennies clean? Why or why not?

   _____

   _____

   _____

   _____

3. Why do you think it would be unwise to clean pennies all the time with vinegar? What might happen to the pennies over time?

   _____

   _____

   _____

   _____

4. What other materials might you try to clean with vinegar?

   _____

   _____

   _____

   _____

DESIGN PROCESS REVIEW—CLEANING PENNIES

Share your journal entries and experiences with your classmates during a discussion led by your teacher.

NAME _____

BOUNCING POPCORN

Directions: Work in teams of two as you perform this activity. Gather these materials as directed by your teacher.

TEAM MATERIALS
- 1-ounce measuring cup
- baking soda
- clear plastic cups or glasses
- food coloring
- light seeds
- straws
- teaspoons
- unpopped popcorn kernels
- vinegar
- watch or stopwatch
- water

GETTING STARTED

1. Pour 4 ounces of water into an 8-ounce clear plastic cup.

2. Pour 2 ounces of vinegar into the clear plastic cup.

3. Place one level teaspoon of baking soda into the plastic cup with the vinegar and water. Describe the results.

_____

_____

4. Place two kernels of popcorn into the water and stir with a straw. Observe the reaction and the behavior of the popcorn kernels. Are they gradually going up and down in the solution? If the popcorn kernels remain on the bottom, add one more ounce of vinegar. If they still do not move, add $\frac{1}{2}$ of a teaspoon of baking soda to the mixture. Stir with the straw. Observe and describe the reaction.

_____

_____

KEEPING THE RECORD

5. Keep a record of the ratio as the kernels begin to rise and fall in the solution. For example, if one kernel is up and one kernel is down, write "1 : 2" with the "1" indicating the number of kernels floating and the "2" representing the total number of kernels. The fractional percentage is represented by $\frac{1}{2}$ and the percentage of kernels floating is 50%.

$1 : 2 = \frac{1}{2} = 50\%$

Add two more kernels of popcorn to the solution. If three kernels are on the top of the water (or nearly so), the ratio is 3 : 4. The fraction is $\frac{3}{4}$. The percentage is 75%.

Observe the rising and falling of the kernels and keep a record every 30 seconds. Create a table like the one on the next page to record your results.

NAME _____

BOUNCING POPCORN

Create your own table or use the one below to record the popcorn activity.

4 BOUNCING POPCORN KERNELS			
# OF FLOATING KERNELS	RATIO	FRACTION	PERCENTAGE

Add one more kernel to the water. Add a pinch of baking soda if the kernels have settled on the bottom and aren't moving. Add an eyedropper full of vinegar if the kernels still haven't left the bottom of the glass.

Make another table the same as the one above (or use the one below) and record these results with five kernels. Record the results every 30 seconds.

5 BOUNCING POPCORN KERNELS			
# OF FLOATING KERNELS	RATIO	FRACTION	PERCENTAGE

 NAME _____

BOUNCING POPCORN

Make another table—or use the one below—and record these results with 10 kernels. Record the results every 30 seconds. (Add a pinch of baking soda and an eyedropper full of vinegar if the kernels get sluggish and don't rise all the way to the top.)

10 BOUNCING POPCORN KERNELS			
# OF FLOATING KERNELS	RATIO	FRACTION	PERCENTAGE

1. What other kinds of seeds or light objects might work with the vinegar and baking soda?

   _____

   _____

2. Add two or three drops of food coloring to your cup with the vinegar and baking soda. Observe the results. Describe what happens and how it affects the solution.

   _____

   _____

3. Try adding two or three other seeds of any size and type. Describe what you added to the solution and record the results. Draw a sketch of your cup and kernels/seeds in the box below.

   _____

 _____

_____

BOUNCING POPCORN

JOURNAL ENTRY

1. What was the most interesting thing you learned doing this activity?

   _____
   _____
   _____

2. How could you use this science activity at home?

   _____
   _____
   _____

3. What math concepts did you learn or review while doing this project?

   _____
   _____
   _____

4. Is there anything you learned in this unit—including the math—that you would like to show your parents? Explain your answer.

   _____
   _____
   _____

5. How would you add to this experiment if you had more time or were working on your own at home?

   _____
   _____
   _____

DESIGN PROCESS REVIEW—BOUNCING POPCORN

Share your journal entries and experiences with your classmates during a discussion led by your teacher.

LIQUID-FUELED ROCKETS

Directions: Work in teams of two as you perform this activity. Gather these materials as directed by your teacher.

TEAM MATERIALS

- 1-ounce measuring cup
- baking soda
- chalk
- empty plastic water bottles
- facial tissues
- fishing line
- masking tape
- meterstick, yardstick, ruler, or measuring tape
- plastic teaspoons
- vinegar
- water
- wine corks

BACKGROUND INFORMATION

Household vinegar and baking soda react with each other to release carbon dioxide, a gas that quickly fills a limited space—such as a water bottle—and builds up to a great intensity. In this activity, vinegar and baking soda will be combined in this way. About 20 to 40 seconds after they are combined, the pressure of the carbon dioxide gas in the bottle pushes the cork out with explosive force. This is a very controlled explosion with most of the force being exerted against the weakest point, which is the cork-rocket at the top of the bottle. The vinegar and baking soda provides the propellant force, or the fuel, which sends the cork rocket into the air.

GETTING STARTED

1. Use a regular plastic water bottle for holding the rocket propellant (vinegar and baking soda mixture).

2. Use a wine bottle cork as the rocket's payload. You may want to decorate the cork with your favorite logo, your initials, and your team name.

3. Make sure that the cork fits firmly and tightly into the bottle opening. (To test this, you can put some water into the bottle, twist on the cork, and make sure that no water is able to escape.)

4. To make the cork fit a little tighter—and to keep the gas from escaping from the bottle before launch—wrap a piece of masking tape around the sides of the cork (but not on the top and bottom).

5. Check again that the cork fits *tightly* in the mouth of the bottle.

6. Remove the cork and shake out any water or material. Make sure the bottle is empty.

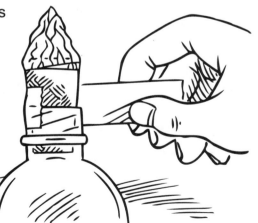

LIQUID-FUELED ROCKETS

MAKING THE PROPELLANT

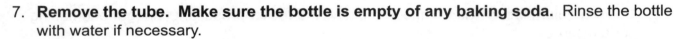

1. Spread open a facial tissue on a dry, clean surface, such as your desk. Use a small measuring cup to pour 30 cc (about 6 teaspoons) of baking soda onto the tissue.

2. Spread out the baking soda in a long row on the tissue. Leave 1 inch of the tissue on each end.

3. Roll the tissue into a long tube with the baking soda spread evenly along the tube.

4. Use three or four pieces of fishing line to tie the baking soda in place in the tissue tube.

5. Tie a 6-inch piece of fishing line to one end of the tube. This will be the top of the tube.

6. Make sure the tube slips easily into the bottle. Pour out any spilled baking soda. Remake the tube if it doesn't fit the bottle, or if the baking soda is spilling out.

7. **Remove the tube. Make sure the bottle is empty of any baking soda.** Rinse the bottle with water if necessary.

8. Make two more tubes in the same way. Make sure the baking soda doesn't spill out. You need three long tubes—each with six teaspoons (30 cc) of baking soda.

9. Pour 4 ounces of vinegar (120 mL) into the bottle.

10. Sketch your rocket in the box below.

LIQUID-FUELED ROCKETS

LAUNCHING YOUR ROCKET

1. Help draw a chalk starting line across an empty playground area free of students.
2. Use yardsticks, metersticks, rulers, or a measuring tape to measure the distance down the side of the launch area.
3. Mark the distances with chalk along both edges of the area or where the distances are clearly visible. Mark the launch areas in meters, yards, or feet.
4. Have paper and pencil to record the distances for your team.

LAUNCH RULES

- Your teacher or a chosen classmate may record distances for the whole class. Teams may also record their own distances.
- You will want to launch the rocket pointed away from you (at about a 45-degree angle) downfield from the starting line. Make sure the bottle stays within 35–50 degrees from the ground.
- You are trying to achieve the greatest distance that can be measured and recorded. (Height can't be easily measured.)

FIRST LAUNCH (4 ounces of vinegar—120 mL)

When it is time for your team to launch, choose one partner to do the first launch. All students should read all instructions before starting.

Follow these steps—carefully:

1. Make sure there are 4 ounces of vinegar in your bottle.
2. Carefully slip the long thin tube into the bottle— **above the vinegar**.
3. Hold the fishing line tied to the tube—**above the vinegar**.
4. Firmly **twist in the cork as tight as you can and point it away immediately**.
5. Aim down the field on the firing range. **Do not look into the bottle top anymore**.

6. Holding the bottle firmly at a **45-degree angle facing away from yourself**, shake until the cork is blown loose by the carbon-dioxide gas. Always point the cork away from yourself and anyone else.

Measure and record your distance for the first launch: _____

LIQUID-FUELED ROCKETS

LAUNCHING YOUR ROCKET

SECOND LAUNCH (5 ounces of vinegar—150 mL)

1. The other partner will launch the rocket this time.

2. Empty the bottle entirely.

3. Pour 5 ounces (150 mL) of vinegar into the bottle.

4. Check your cork. Use another layer of masking tape to cover the cork, if necessary. Make sure the cork fits tightly.

5. Remove the cork and load your second baking soda tube at the top as you did in the first launch.

Replace the cork. Aim your bottle rocket launcher away from yourself at a 45-degree angle. Shake the bottle vigorously until you feel the bottle expand. Always point the cork away from yourself and anyone else. Then, hold steady until the cork is launched.

Measure and record your distance for the second launch: _____

FINAL LAUNCH (6 ounces of vinegar—180 mL)

1. Flip a coin to see who will launch the rocket.

2. Empty the bottle entirely.

3. Pour 6 ounces (180 mL) of vinegar into the bottle.

4. Check your cork. Replace the layer of masking tape to cover the cork if necessary. Make sure the cork fits tightly. Insert your third baking soda tube as before.

5. Aim your bottle rocket launcher at a 45-degree angle away from yourself.

6. Shake the bottle and hold it steady until the cork is launched. Always point the cork away from yourself and anyone else.

Measure and record your distance for the third launch: _____

 _____

LIQUID-FUELED ROCKETS

JOURNAL ENTRY

1. Which launch was your most successful? Explain why.

   _____

   _____

   _____

2. What was the greatest difficulty you faced in making your rocket launcher work correctly? Explain the difficulty.

   _____

   _____

   _____

3. What might you try to make your rocket go farther? What different materials might work better?

   _____

   _____

   _____

4. How could you launch a cork rocket with more propellant (vinegar and baking soda)? What other materials would need to use greater amounts?

   _____

   _____

   _____

5. What was the best part of this project?

   _____

   _____

   _____

DESIGN PROCESS REVIEW—LIQUID-FUELED ROCKETS

Share your journal entries and experiences with your classmates during a discussion led by your teacher.

KITCHEN CHEMISTS

CHALLENGE ACTIVITY—DESIGN YOUR OWN EXPERIMENT

Work in teams of two to design and conduct your own experiment using the materials available in the previous activities. Your experiment can build on the one of the previous activities or can be an entirely new experiment. Use the Design Process Worksheet on page 5 to help guide your work. Get teacher approval before beginning your experiment.

TEAM MATERIALS
- 1-ounce (30 cc) measuring cups
- baking soda
- chalk
- corks
- eggs or eggshells
- empty water bottles
- eyedroppers
- facial tissue
- fishing line
- magnifying glasses
- paper towels
- pennies and other coins
- popping corn
- small cups (1 oz. and 6 oz.)
- small rocks
- turkey or chicken bones
- vinegar
- yardsticks, metersticks, rulers, or measuring tape

SUGGESTIONS:

1. Create a better, bigger, more powerful rocket.

2. Find another type of coin or metal to clean as you did the pennies.

3. Find a lightly rusted tool or toy to clean as you did the pennies.

4. Find old bones to turn into "rubber" bones.

5. Find eggshells to make disappear.

6. Make bigger seeds (and smaller ones) bounce.

7. Try a broken seashell or similar material in a vinegar bath.

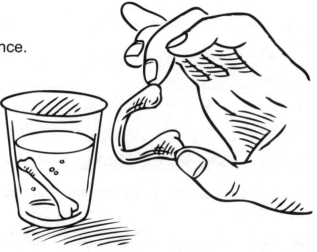

 NAME _____

KITCHEN CHEMISTS

CHALLENGE ACTIVITY—DESIGN YOUR OWN EXPERIMENT

Your Topic: _____

What You Hope to Accomplish: _____

_____

_____

Your Procedure:

Step 1: _____

_____

Step 2: _____

_____

Step 3: _____

_____

Step 4: _____

_____

(Add more steps on the back of this page if needed.)

Your Results: _____

_____

_____

Sketch the setup of your experiment in the box below.

 _____

KITCHEN CHEMISTS

CHALLENGE ACTIVITY—JOURNAL ENTRY

Use a computer, tablet, or other device to answer each paragraph subject below. Be sure to use paragraph format and complete sentences.

PARAGRAPH 1

How would you make a rubber bone or dissolve an eggshell for your parents or younger siblings? Provide explicit details in terms of materials used, the amounts of materials (even water), and the process of adding or combining materials. (You may refer to your activity notes.)

PARAGRAPH 2

How would you clean several rusted, old pennies you found in a garden?

PARAGRAPH 3

What would you do to make popcorn, bean seeds, and pea seeds bounce in a cup of water?

PARAGRAPH 4

How would you fire a vinegar-and-baking-soda rocket to get maximum distance?

PARAGRAPH 5

Respond to the question by referring back to the activities you completed in this unit.

1. *How do vinegar and baking soda react when you mix them together?*
2. *What are some of the uses of chemistry that you can do at home and at school?*
3. *What is needed to make a controlled rocket using vinegar and baking soda?*
4. *How can you clean and shine coins at home?*
5. *How can you make bones act like rubber?*

DESIGN PROCESS REVIEW—KITCHEN CHEMISTS

Share your chemistry experiments and results with your classmates in the class discussion/presentations your teacher leads to culminate this unit.

FLYING SAUCERS

> **4 Sessions:** 1 session per each activity (approximately 1 to $1\frac{1}{2}$ hours per session)

CONNECTIONS AND SUGGESTIONS

SCIENCE—Students will be building flying saucers and other flying objects out of manila folders and tagboard. Activities will involve properties of flight, the influence of wind, and creative efforts to get objects airborne.

TECHNOLOGY—The primary technology in this unit is the creation of a variety of flying disks that are adaptable to several different wind conditions (including none at all). For this project, students can use basic computer software to write a brief report in which they describe the problems encountered, the solutions attempted, the success rate of each activity, the different approaches used, and any suggestions for improvement. The final journal entry can also be used for students to evaluate the project.

ENGINEERING—Students will experiment with a variety of engineering designs and the listed materials to create flying saucers and objects. The emphasis will be on distance and behavior of the flying objects in various wind conditions.

MATH—Students will use their understanding of geometry—the area of a circle and triangle—to compute the area of their own flying creations. They will also measure distances.

Materials

- brads
- glue or rubber cement
- large and small paper clips
- manila folders, Bristol board, or tagboard
- markers
- math compasses
- pennies
- plastic covers for margarine containers; water-bottle caps; or similar round, light, plastic or Styrofoam™ objects

- push pins
- rulers
- scissors
- scratch paper
- small plastic cups
- tape
- yardsticks and/or metersticks

UNIT 6 VOCABULARY

airfoil—a surface (such as a wing) designed to aid in lifting or controlling an aircraft by making use of air currents

area—the number of unit squares in a flat shape—often measured in square inches or square feet

capsule—a detachable compartment on a flying object

circumference—the distance around the outer edge of a circle

diameter—the distance across a circle through the center of the circle

disk—a round, flat object

dome—a round, three-dimensional fixture on a structure—often shaped like a half of a sphere

engineer—an individual who plans and builds structures

evaluate—to make a judgment

observations—scientific information observed during an experiment

perimeter—the distance around an object

pi (3.14)—the relationship of the circumference of a circle to the diameter

radius—the distance from the center of the circle to the edge

ratio—relationship between two numbers written as "2:3" or said as "2 to 3"

reinforce—to support or strengthen

DISCUSSION PROMPT:

Flying saucers are most often the subject of science fiction, complete with aliens that have things like tentacles, 10 eyes, and four mouths. NASA, however, is bringing science fiction to life as it is planning the launch of a flying saucer! Called a Low-Density Supersonic Decelerator (LDSD), the shape of the spacecraft allows for it to decrease aerodynamic efficiency. This means the shape will actually slow the vehicle down instead of speeding it up. Why do you think astronauts would want their vehicle to move slower rather than faster?

FLYING SAUCERS

A flying saucer (also known as a flying disc) is a term used for any flying object that is out of the norm. Often people attach theories to sightings of saucers that they are extraterrestrial and come from outer space. The term was coined in 1947, after a highly publicized sighting where the witnesses described what they saw as looking like "a saucer, disc, or pie plate." The United States Air Force officially changed the term to "unidentified flying object" or "UFO" in 1952. While many of the thousands of saucer/UFO sightings are believed to be hoaxes, there are some man-made saucer-like crafts. Disc-shaped aircraft have been developed since before World War II. In fact, NASA has recently been working on a saucer-shaped craft in order to be able to land in Mars' extremely thin atmosphere.

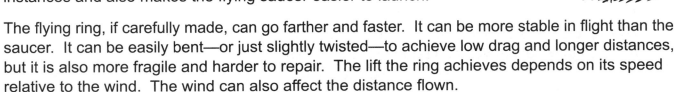

The flying disk built in this activity is basically an airfoil. An airfoil is the most basic shape of a wing used on most aircrafts. Aircrafts use airfoils to achieve lift by directing air downward. By bending the outer lip or edge of the flying saucer downward, you will find that the saucer usually rises higher and flies farther than the straight flying saucer. The wind conditions at the time of launch will also affect the flight characteristics. In some wind conditions, just a slight downward curve in the shape of the saucer will result in much longer flights. The gradually rising center of the flying saucer can create lift and increase distance in many instances and also makes the flying saucer easier to launch.

The flying ring, if carefully made, can go farther and faster. It can be more stable in flight than the saucer. It can be easily bent—or just slightly twisted—to achieve low drag and longer distances, but it is also more fragile and harder to repair. The lift the ring achieves depends on its speed relative to the wind. The wind can also affect the distance flown.

The flying triangle can be erratic. It depends on the wind conditions and the carefulness of construction. It often serves as a contrast for the faster circular objects, illustrating the advantage of the circular shape.

Use a computer or tablet to search for information on the Internet to help you as you complete the activities in this unit. Helpful search terms include:

| airfoil | disc | flying saucers | hover | propulsion | thrust |

 _____

MAKING A FLYING SAUCER

Directions: Work in teams of two as you perform this first activity. Gather these materials as instructed by your teacher.

TEAM MATERIALS

- brads
- large and small paper clips
- manila folders, Bristol board, or tagboard
- markers

- math compasses
- push pins
- rulers
- scratch paper

- scissors
- tape, glue, or rubber cement
- thin stirrer or brush
- yardstick or meterstick

NOTE: Practice with the math compass on scratch paper before working on the manila folders, especially if you have not used compasses before. It takes some dexterity to use a compass effectively. Holding the pencil end lightly while smoothly rotating the compass is tricky. You may find it easier or more efficient to rotate the paper rather than the compass.

GETTING STARTED

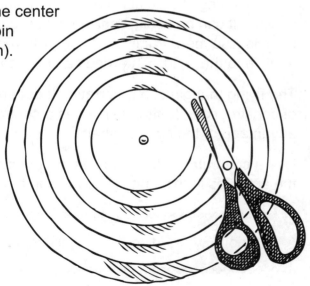

1. Use a math compass to make the first circle on a manila folder, piece of tagboard, or piece of Bristol board. Set the compass for 4 inches (10 cm), which will provide a 4-inch (10 cm) radius and an 8-inch (20 cm) diameter across the center of the circle. Remember to lightly turn the compass as you make this first circle. Mark the center of the circle and use a push pin to make a small hole. Cut out the circle carefully.

2. Use the compass to make a second circle on another folder. Set a radius of 3.5 inches (9 cm). Cut out this circle as well. Use the push pin to make a hole in the center of this circle.

3. Use the compass to measure four more circles with radii of 3 inches (7.5 cm), 2.5 inches (6.25 cm), 2 inches (5 cm), and 1.5 inches (3.75 cm). Use the push pin to make holes in the center of each disk where the sharp point of the compass was set.

4. Line up the disks on the push pin and enlarge the center holes slightly so that you can replace the push pin with a paper fastener (brad—$\frac{3}{4}$ or 1 inch in length). Leave the brad loose for a moment and place glue or rubber cement between each circle. Spread out the glue or rubber cement with a thin stirrer, brush, or your finger. Tape can also be used.

5. Firmly press along your disk and tighten the brad by bending it across the bottom layer.

MAKING A FLYING SAUCER

GETTING STARTED *(cont.)*

6. Reset your math compass to the 4-inch setting you used for the largest circle. Place the compass point on any point along the edge of the largest disk. Make a dot.

7. Don't change the compass setting. Draw an arc from that dot—it will cross the edge of this large disk. Put a dot where this arc crosses the edge of the disk. Don't change the compass setting. Follow the same procedure around the outside edge of the disk.

8. You should have evenly spaced dots along the edge of the circle. (All circles have 360 degrees. Six arcs evenly spaced are 60 degrees each.)

ADDING WEIGHT

Place one large paper clip at each of the six dots. Each paper clip firmly holds the layers of the flying saucer together. Use a piece of masking tape on the bottom of the saucer to fix each of the six paper clips in place. Place a piece of masking tape over the blades of the center brad as well.

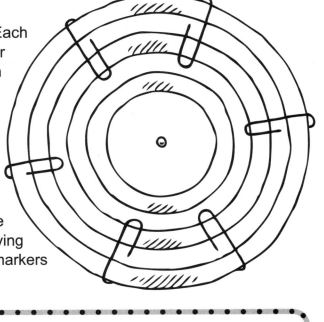

ADD COLOR

You will want to decorate your flying saucer with bright colors and possibly a design, which will make it easier to recognize the saucer when you are retrieving it. Be creative. Name your saucer and write it with markers on the bottom of the saucer.

LAUNCHING THE FLYING SAUCER

These flying saucers work best on a nice open field or playground. You will launch the flying saucer with a quick snap of the wrist, just as you would throw a Frisbee®. Note how it flies. Some will flip over and fly upside down. Some will hit the air currents and make sudden shifts in direction. Many will reach a height well above the field and sail for a distance before landing. You may also find that sometimes you can hold the saucer in a vertical position and flip it up in the air, where it will catch the wind and flatten out.

Sketch your flying saucer in flight in the box to the right.

 NAME _____

MAKING A FLYING SAUCER

MEASURING DISTANCES

Use a yardstick and/or meterstick to measure the distance from your launching place to the point where the flying saucer landed. Record the distance to the nearest yard or meter. Launch three flights and record the distances below

Flight # 1: _____ yards/meters (*circle one*)

Flight # 2: _____ yards/meters (*circle one*)

Flight # 3: _____ yards/meters (*circle one*)

Save your flying saucer for work in later units and for flight comparisons.

FLYING MATH

To compute the area of your flying saucer, use this formula: Area = **pi** (π) times the **radius** (r) squared ($A = π × r^2$). The area is the amount of flat space on the circular disk. The radius is the distance from the center to the edge of the disk. **Pi** is represented by 3.14. The radius of a circle that is 6 inches from side-to-side through the middle of the circle, would be 3 inches.

The formula is computed as A = 3.14 × 3 × 3. This is 3.14 × 9 = 28.26 square inches. The area of this circle is 28.26 in^2.

Compute the area of your flying saucer here:

radius = _____ inches (or cm)

pi = 3.14

A = 3.14 × _____ × _____

Area = _____ inches² (or cm²)

Compute the area of a flying saucer with a radius of 5 centimeters.

A = 3.14 × _____ × _____

A = _____ cm²

Making a Flying Saucer

Journal Entry

1. How did your flying saucer work? Did it rise and then level out? Did it fly a great distance? How did it react in the wind?

   _____

   _____

   _____

2. Did you and your partner add any special touches to your saucer that may have affected its performance?

   _____

   _____

   _____

3. What changes would you add to your flying saucer to improve its flight?

   _____

   _____

   _____

4. What do you think would happen if the center was removed or if the saucer was shaped like an "O"?

   _____

   _____

   _____

5. What could you place on top of the saucer in the center if you were improving or experimenting with your flying saucer?

   _____

   _____

   _____

Design Process Review—Making a Flying Saucer

Share your journal entries and flying saucers with your classmates during a discussion led by your teacher.

MAKING A DOMED SAUCER

Directions: Work in teams of two as you perform this activity. Gather these materials as instructed by your teacher.

TEAM MATERIALS
- brads
- large and small paper clips
- manila folders, Bristol board, or tagboard
- math compasses
- plastic or Styrofoam™ objects such as water-bottle caps, cups, or similar round, light objects
- push pins
- scissors
- small plastic cups
- rulers
- tape, glue, or rubber cement

1. Use your flying saucer from the previous unit as your base model. Repair any parts that are damaged or need replacement. Make sure the paper clips are in place and taped down.

2. Make a dome by mounting a small plastic cup in the center of your flying saucer. (If you'd like, cut a couple of paper figures as riders in the dome.) Use masking tape or clear plastic tape to mount the dome securely on the top center of your flying saucer. Sketch your domed saucer in the box below.

3. Launch this saucer with a strong flick of the wrist or try a long launch across the body.

4. Once you get the domed saucer in the air, observe its flight characteristics. Does it fly as far or as high as the original saucer?   **YES   NO**

   Do several launches. Which method works best?

   _____

   _____

5. Choose a different dome-shaped capsule to add on your flying saucer. Try a Styrofoam™ cup cut down to half-size, a plastic bottle cap, or a similar object. Load up your flying saucer, tape it securely and launch this new capsule.

   Which material worked best? Why? Describe your results for the materials you used.

   _____

   _____

MAKING A DOMED SAUCER

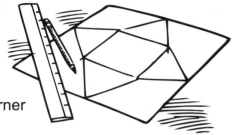

6. Try this capsule. Use a manila folder or tagboard—about 6 inches square—as the base. Use a ruler to measure a 3-inch square in the center of the 6-inch square. Use your math compass to form a triangle along each of the four sides outside the square. See the figure to the right. The triangles are formed by drawing an arc from each corner on each side of the 3-inch square.

7. Cut away the extra material. Fold each triangle over the 3-inch square and tape them in place to create a four-sided pyramid for the top of your saucer.

8. Tape your triangle to the flying saucer and do several trials. Sketch your saucer in the box below.

9. Were you able to get your saucer airborne? Which way did it fly—upright, upside down, or both?

_____

_____

_____

MAKING A DOMED SAUCER

JOURNAL ENTRY

1. Which of your domed flying-saucer styles worked best for you today? Why?

   _____

   _____

   _____

2. What would happen if you had two capsules on your flying saucer? Do you think it would fly? How would the two capsules—one on each side of the saucer—affect the flight characteristics of the saucer? Explain your answer and your reasoning.

   _____

   _____

   _____

3. Why is it so important to measure carefully and to securely attach the capsules?

   _____

   _____

   _____

4. What was the best idea you observed on someone else's flying saucer? Why was it such a good idea?

   _____

   _____

   _____

5. What would you do differently next time if you were doing this activity again? Explain your answer.

   _____

   _____

   _____

DESIGN PROCESS REVIEW—MAKING A DOMED SAUCER

Share your journal entries, domed saucers, and observations with your classmates during a discussion led by your teacher.

FLYING RINGS

Directions: Work in teams of two as you perform this activity. Gather these materials as instructed by your teacher.

TEAM MATERIALS

- large and small paper clips
- manila folders, Bristol board, or tagboard
- math compasses

- pennies
- scissors
- stickers and/or markers (optional)
- rulers

- tape, glue, or rubber cement
- yardstick or meterstick

MAKING THE RING

1. On a piece of manila folder, thick Bristol board, or tagboard, set the math compass for a 4-inch (10 cm) radius to draw a circle with an 8-inch (20 cm) diameter.

2. On the same folder or board, move the compass setting to a 2-inch (5 cm) radius. Draw this radius inside the larger circle. Cut out the inner circle, but be careful to keep the outer circle intact. Save this inner circle for making small flying saucers later.

3. Cut out the outer circle so that you have a ring with a large opening.

4. On another piece of folder or board, set the math compass for a 3.5-inch (8.75 cm) radius to draw a circle with a 7-inch (17.5 cm) diameter.

5. On the same folder or board, move the compass setting to a 2-inch (5 cm) radius. Draw this radius inside the 7-inch (17.5 cm) radius. Cut out the inner circle and keep the outer circle intact. Save the inner circle for making small flying saucers later.

6. Cut out the outer circle so that you have a thin ring that fits over the one you cut before. It should fit so that the second ring reinforces the first ring. Glue the upper smaller ring onto the wider one you made first.

7. Set the compass to 60 degrees. Mark a dot on the outer edge of the ring. Place the compass point on that dot and make an arc. Make a dot where the arc crosses the outer edge of the ring, then move the compass point to that dot and make a new arc. Keep the same 60-degree compass setting for each arc. Repeat this until you have six evenly spaced dots around the edge of the ring.

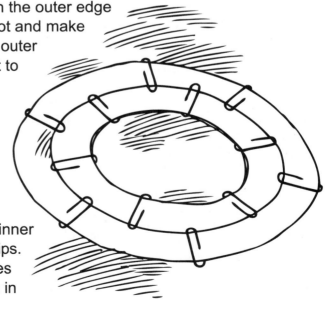

8. Place one large paper clip at each dot on the outer edge of the ring. It will help hold the upper ring in place as well.

9. Place a second circle of paper clips along the inner edge of the circle between each pair of outer clips. This reinforces the strength of ring and provides added weight to the ring. Tape the paper clips in place with clear tape or masking tape.

 **NAME** _____

FLYING RINGS

LAUNCHING THE RING

Like the flying saucers, these flying rings are launched with a swift snap of the wrist as you turn your body. After that, the wind conditions determine how long and how far the ring will fly. Some sail across a playground. Some will fall quite quickly. Some rings change their direction and slowly, gently land downfield. Usually, you will get more distance if you wait for a gentle breeze and launch into the direction the wind is moving. A good overhand throw or a sidearm toss are both effective.

Use a yardstick or meterstick to measure the distance from your launching place to the point where the flying ring landed. Record the distance to the nearest yard or meter. Launch three flights and record the distances below.

Flight # 1: _____ yards/meters (*circle one*)

Flight # 2: _____ yards/meters (*circle one*)

Flight # 3: _____ yards/meters (*circle one*)

USE UNBALANCED RINGS

One way to experiment with your ring is to change the weight distribution. This works well in some gusty wind conditions. Remove some of the inner and outer paper clips and rearrange them so that one side of the saucer is a little heavier than the other. You will want to keep at least a third of the paper clips on the now-lighter side. Arrange the clips you removed between the ones on the other side of the ring. Don't forget to tape down the paper clips. Experiment with different arrangements until you find one that works best for you.

ON YOUR OWN

Make your next ring according to your own design. Try entirely different paper clip arrangements. Tape on pennies instead of paper clips or try taping pennies *over* paper clips. Consider other possible weights that are safe to use. You may use stickers or markers to decorate your flying ring. Sketch your design in the box.

FLYING RINGS

JOURNAL ENTRY

1. Which ring or weight arrangement worked best for you? Why?

   _____

   _____

   _____

2. Which weather conditions (breezes, strong wind, gusty wind, very little wind, other conditions) were the best or most effective when you launched your flying ring?

   _____

   _____

   _____

3. What would you change about the ring design—in terms of added features, weights, shapes, or other designs—if you were making another ring?

   _____

   _____

   _____

4. Explain why you think the ring was able to fly without the center other saucers had.

   _____

   _____

   _____

5. How do you think a triangular "ring" would fly? What advantages or disadvantages would the triangular shape have?

   _____

   _____

   _____

DESIGN PROCESS REVIEW—FLYING RINGS

Share your journal entries, flying rings, and observations with your classmates during a discussion led by your teacher.

FLYING VEHICLES

CHALLENGE ACTIVITY—CREATE YOUR OWN FLYING SAUCER

TEAM MATERIALS

- brads
- large and small paper clips
- manila folders, Bristol board, or tagboard
- masking tape
- push pins
- rulers
- scissors
- tape, glue, or rubber cement
- yardstick or meterstick

You have been working with solid flying saucers, flying rings, and domed flying saucers, which you built following directions. Consider the best model you made of a flying saucer, a domed saucer, or a ring of any dimensions. This is your opportunity to create the best model possible of any of these flying objects. You can alter dimensions, measurements, designs, arrangements, colors, weights or other specifications as you wish. Use the Design Process Worksheet on page 5 to help guide your work. You will also keep a specification sheet for the model you build. Complete it as you finish your model.

CHOICES TO CONSIDER

- Regular flying saucer
- Domed saucer
- Diamond domed saucer
- Flying ring
- Flying triangle (next page)

RULES

1. The project must not exceed 12 inches in diameter (distance across the center). (Smaller saucers have much better chances of working.)

2. You must use the available materials.

3. Use reasonable amounts of glue, tape, rubber cement, folders, and other materials.

4. Share tools and materials.

ⓃⒶⓂⒺ _____

FLYING VEHICLES

CHALLENGE ACTIVITY—CREATE YOUR OWN FLYING SAUCER

MAKING FLYING TRIANGLES

1. Measure carefully and cut nine strips of tagboard, Bristol board, or manila folders with these dimensions:
    a. three strips that are each $2\frac{1}{2}$ inches (6.5 cm) wide and 8 inches (20 cm) long
    b. three strips that are each 2 inches (5 cm) wide and 8 inches (20 cm) long
    c. three strips that are each 1 inch (2.5 cm) wide and 8 inches (20 cm) long.

2. Carefully glue each 1-inch-wide strip on top of one 2-inch strip.

3. Carefully glue each double strip on top of one of the 2.5-inch strips.

4. Carefully glue (or rubber cement) the ends of the three widest ($2\frac{1}{2}$ inch) strips together to form a triangle.

5. Use a push pin to make a hole at each corner in the triangle. Insert one brad into each of the holes. Fold the brad down and cover each corner with a piece of masking tape.

6. Arrange two large paper clips on each side of the triangle. Fit them tightly. Make sure they are spread apart to distribute the weight. Attach them securely with a piece of masking tape.

LAUNCHING THE TRIANGULAR RING

Like the flying saucers, these triangular flying rings are launched with a swift snap of the wrist as you turn your body. After that, the wind conditions determine how long and how far the ring will fly. You will usually get more distance, if you wait for a gentle breeze and launch in the direction the wind is moving. A good overhand throw or a sidearm toss is effective.

LAUNCHING THE DISK

Launch the triangular ring and compare distances with your rings and original flying saucers. Record the distances here in yards or meters from the point where you launched.

1st trial: _____ yards/meters (*circle one*)

2nd trial: _____ yards/meters (*circle one*)

3rd trial: _____ yards/meters (*circle one*)

MAKING ADJUSTMENTS

Sometimes the triangular pieces don't stay together as well as you would like or the wind isn't strong enough for the ring. Place your triangular ring on a piece of tagboard or a manila folder. Draw an outline of the edge of your triangle ring. Cut out this piece and glue it securely to the bottom of the ring. Use the paper clips to attach to this base and tape the paper clips on as well.

FLYING VEHICLES

CHALLENGE ACTIVITY—CREATE YOUR OWN FLYING SAUCER

TRIANGULAR MATH

Compute the area of your triangle.

Use a ruler to measure the height of the triangle in centimeters.

Height = _____ cm

Use a ruler to measure the base of the triangle in centimeters.

Base = _____ cm

The formula for the area of a triangle is $\frac{1}{2}$ the base times the height. $A = \frac{1}{2}b \times h$.

For example, a triangle with a 10-cm height and an 8-inch base would have the following equation:

$\frac{1}{2} \times 10 \times 8 = 5 \times 8 = 40$ cm^2

Your dimensions: $\frac{1}{2} \times$ _____ $\times$ _____ $=$ _____ cm^2

Sketch your triangular ring in the box below.

FLYING VEHICLES

CHALLENGE ACTIVITY—CREATE YOUR OWN FLYING SAUCER

SPECIFICATION PAGE (for flying triangle or other models you created)

Project Name: _____

Description of Vehicle: _____

_____

Materials Used: _____

_____

Test Results: (Did it fly? How far did it fly, in feet or yards?)

_____

_____

_____

Best Feature of Your Model

_____

_____

_____

Your Illustration of the Model

FLYING VEHICLES

CHALLENGE ACTIVITY—JOURNAL ENTRY

Use a computer, tablet, or other device to answer each paragraph subject below. Be sure to use paragraph format and complete sentences.

PARAGRAPH 1

Which of the rings or saucers you made in any of the activities flew the farthest? Why? Why did that design work best?

PARAGRAPH 2

By doing this activity, what did you learn about air movement, flight, and flying objects?

PARAGRAPH 3

Which of the rings or saucers had the most erratic flight and/or unpredictable landing places? What was special, different, interesting, and unusual about it? Describe the behavior of the disk that was different.

PARAGRAPH 4

Respond to these questions by referring back to the activities you completed in this unit.

1. *How can you make a well-balanced, effective circular flying object?*
2. *How large and heavy a flying object did you design, create, and fly?*
3. *What effect did wind have on the flying object?*
4. *How did the differently designed flying objects behave in the air?*
5. *What is the most effective design and construction for circular flying objects?*
6. *If you made a triangular flying object, how did it behave in the air?*

DESIGN PROCESS REVIEW—FLYING VEHICLES

Share your saucers, journal entries, and experiences with your classmates in the class discussion/presentations your teacher leads to culminate this unit.

 **7**

DERBY CARS

> **4 Sessions:** 1 session per each activity (approximately 1 to $1\frac{1}{2}$ hours per session)

CONNECTIONS AND SUGGESTIONS

SCIENCE—Students will learn methods for using motion and momentum. They will learn how to reduce friction. They will learn ways to take advantage of load placement to increase speed. Students will learn to use terms such as *speed*, *velocity*, and *acceleration*. They will learn how to measure speed in terms of meters per second and convert it into miles per hour. Students will learn about and apply Newton's Three Laws of Motion in a variety of activities.

TECHNOLOGY—Students will develop vehicles by using techniques used to increase speed, reduce friction, and utilize gravity to increase momentum. Students may use small motors to propel their vehicles. (Teachers—or students—can find these mini-motors in science kits, school science supply houses, from Internet sources, and in electronics stores.) Timing and measurement instruments will be used. Students can research model cars, soap-box racers, and racing information on the Internet.

ENGINEERING—Students will use simple, easily available materials such as sign boards, stirrers, straws, water bottle caps, coffee lids, wooden skewers, poster board, and many other objects to create small vehicles. A cafeteria table with folding legs works as the initial ramp. Students will experiment with methods and objects that provide sturdy vehicles, greater momentum, various levels of friction, different loads, strength, durability, and other factors.

MATH—Students will work with a variety of measurement devices and applications, and they will learn formulas and apply ratios related to speed, distance, and weight.

Materials

This is a list of suggested materials. Display these materials in the classroom to stimulate students' ideas for bringing their own materials from home. Encourage students to bring in objects and materials that they think will be of good use when making their roller derby cars.

- 1.5 volt motors with 2 wire leads
- barbecue skewers/nails (for making holes)
- batteries
- battery holders (or rubber bands)
- colored markers
- food boxes (such as cereal and cracker boxes)
- index cards
- lids from coffee cans, margarine tubs, etc.
- math compass

- milk cartons
- paper clips
- pencils
- postal scale (or other weighing device)
- push pins
- rubber bands
- rulers
- sandpaper
- scissors

- scissors
- small pieces of wood
- stiff cardboard
- stiff wire
- straws
- watch/stopwatch
- water bottles
- wooden dowels
- yardstick/meterstick

Suggested Materials

- checkers
- coffee lids or drink lids
- craft sticks
- film canisters and lids

- juice or water-bottle caps
- manila envelopes/poster board/tagboard
- plastic cups

- Styrofoam™
- tape (masking/Scotch/duct)
- thin plastic stirrers
- yogurt lids

· UNIT 7 VOCABULARY ·

acceleration—the increase in the rate of speed of an object in motion

axle—a pole or bar on which a wheel revolves

direction—the line along which an object moves or point it is moving toward

friction—the rubbing of one object against another—a force that slows or prevents the movement of an object

momentum—the force of a moving object; the product of the mass of an object times its velocity

resistance—a force (like friction) that acts to slow or prevent movement of an object

speed—how fast an object moves, measured by the distance traveled in a period of time

spoiler—a device to change air flow in order to increase speed or efficiency in automobiles

traction—the power of an object to hold a surface without slipping

velocity—the speed of an object moving in one direction in a period of time

wheel—a disk or circular frame that can turn on a central point

DISCUSSION PROMPT:

Derby cars originated from the Pinewood Derby®, a racing event in which Cub Scouts are given blocks of wood made of pine, four wheels, and four nails. The scout has to use all nine pieces and can carve, shape, and decorate the wood however he sees fit. Can you think of any other situations in which someone takes a shapeless block of material and turns it into something else entirely? What about an example of a person using old or recycled materials to create something new?

DERBY CARS

Model derby cars (similar to the ones you'll be building in this unit) became popular with the start of the Pinewood Derby®. A Cub Scout Master in 1953 wanted to create a new father-son activity to do with his 10-year-old son who was too young to race in the Soap Box Derby. Soapbox cars were originally made from wooden soap crates and roller-skate wheels. Soapbox cars are also known as gravity racers, as they are motorless and require the driver to drive the car down a hill, propelled by gravity. They can achieve speeds of up to 70 miles per hour.

The Pinewood Derby uses miniature cars made from pine wood, plastic wheels, and metal axles. The accelerating force is gravity, and the opposing forces are friction and air drag. Car modifications aim at maximizing the potential energy in the car design and minimizing the opposing forces. Some builders sand or polish the wheels' tread to reduce friction, and others raise the front wheels slightly to reduce rolling resistance. You can consider many different modifications for your derby car to increase its speed.

The Pinewood Derby became so popular that the races have expanded to include a "raingutter regatta" with boats and a "space derby" using rubber-band powered rockets. Another type of derby is a demolition derby, which uses full-sized, motorized vehicles. This type of derby strays from the original aim in that the cars used are not built for speed. In fact, the areas in which they hold the derbies are usually dirt tracks or fields soaked in water. This causes the area to become muddy, which purposely slows down the vehicles. The racers do not race against each other, but rather aim specifically at destroying each other's cars. While this can be quite a dangerous sport and is not recommended for use in this unit, you might find some fun examples for decorating your derby car. Part of the appeal of the demolition derby cars is the wild and creative paint jobs and designs.

The cars you will create in this unit will be made from common materials and can be modified as you experiment with speed and momentum. You can consider different sizes and numbers of wheels, axle sizes, and ways to power your car.

Use a computer or tablet to search for information on the Internet to help you as you complete the activities in this unit. Look at videos on YouTube for tutorials on building derby cars. Helpful search terms include:

acceleration	friction	momentum	soapbox racers	velocity
aerodynamic	model cars	Pinewood Derby	speed	

MAKING A RACER

Directions: Work in teams of two as you perform this first activity. Gather these materials as instructed by your teacher.

SUGGESTED TOOLS FOR THIS PROJECT:

- colored markers
- math compasses
- pencils
- postal scale (or other weighing device)

- push pins
- rulers
- sandpaper (for smoothing surfaces)
- scissors

- watch or stopwatch
- wooden barbecue skewers, nails, pencils, or pens (for making holes)
- yardstick (or meterstick)

SUGGESTED MATERIALS FOR THIS PROJECT:

- craft sticks
- coffee or drink lids
- corks
- plastic water bottles
- manila envelopes, poster board, tagboard, or any similar material

- margarine cups or lids
- masking tape, Scotch tape, or duct tape
- paper clips
- regular plastic straws
- small boxes or cartons (such as food or check boxes)

- small wood pieces
- Styrofoam™
- thin plastic straw stirrers
- water-bottle caps
- wooden dowels

CONSTRUCTION TIPS

Successful derby cars are produced by careful and accurate work and precise measurements. Effective construction is produced by the following actions:

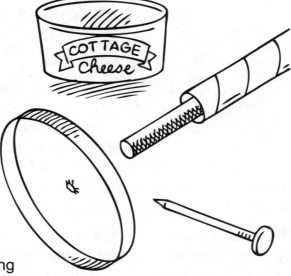

1. Make the holes in the wheels very tight to avoid slippage of the axles.

2. When choosing a material to make the axle, choose something thin and sturdy. Make sure the axle is thin enough that a straw with a wider diameter can fit over it and allow for easy, fast, smooth movement. This wider straw that the axle will spin is called the *axle housing*.

3. Make sure tape does not catch against any moving parts—such as the axles or wheels.

4. Make sure the car box is not so long, wide, or high that it is slowed down by air resistance, weight, height, or other factors.

MAKING A RACER

GETTING STARTED—THE BASIC BODY

Don't make the basic body of your racer too big or too small to start with. A check box, a small milk carton, and a fast-food container are good-sized objects for the basic body. Any box about 6 to 8 inches long and 2 to 4 inches wide is ideal. Make any modifications and decorations for the box after you have attached the wheels and axles.

You can also use a flat piece of thin balsa wood; a thin piece of pine wood; a wood shingle; or a small, slender piece of plywood to make the racer body. A very stiff piece of cardboard or a block of Styrofoam™ packing can also work as the body of the racer. A piece of corrugated plastic is excellent. Side materials for the body can be made from index cards and similar, less sturdy materials.

WHEELS

You can use many round objects for wheels. Try these:

- checkers
- film canister lids
- hot drink lids
- juice caps
- margarine tub lids
- plastic cups
- water bottle caps
- yogurt lids

NOTE: The front and back wheels don't have to be the same size or the same materials.

WHEEL MODELS

Below are some examples of wheel models you can use for your racer.

MAKING A RACER

REINFORCING THE WHEELS

1. You can reinforce thin drink lids by cutting a disk of cardboard, tagboard, or manila folder to fit the size of the lid.

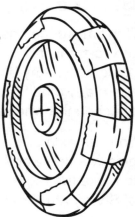

2. Fit the disk between two lids to make a much sturdier wheel.

3. The lids can face either toward each other or away from each other with the disk between the lids. If you need to increase wheel traction for motorized vehicles, use masking tape to connect the pieces around the outside—like tires on a wheel.

WHEELS AND AXLES

This is a critical part of the project. The easiest and most efficient systems use wheel and axle units where the wheel and axle are hooked together in one unit. For the axle, use a thin, stiff straw or a wood barbecue skewer. The straw or skewer should be 6 to 10 inches long. (Don't adjust the length until your car is nearly finished.)

MAKING STRONGER AXLES

To make a straw axle even stronger so that it will wear longer and hold a heavier car, reinforce the straw. Slit another straw of the same size down the length of the straw. Slide the slit straw inside the first straw or wrap it around the first straw if the slit straw won't fit inside. If you wish, use a thin wood dowel or a skewer for the axle. Fit the dowel, skewer, or straw tightly into the cap or lid (wheel).

CONNECTING THE WHEELS

1. Use a push pin or something with a sharp point to make a small hole in the lid, cap, or other round object you are using for a wheel. Be sure to make the hole in the center of the lid.

2. Make the hole slightly larger, if needed, by inserting the point of a pen or pencil, a compass point, or the sharp end of one scissor blade into the hole made by the push pin.

MAKING A RACER

FITTING THE WHEEL AND AXLE

Try fitting the axle into the wheel. You want the axle to just fit through the hole and fit snugly. The tighter it fits, the better it will work.

TESTING THE WHEEL AND AXLE

When you turn the axle, the wheel should turn, too. If you twirl the axle with your thumb and forefinger, the whole unit should whirl around freely.

ATTACHING THE WHEEL, THE AXLE, AND THE AXLE HOUSING

1. Attach only one wheel to the axle.
2. Obtain a large straw with a diameter wider than the axle you just made.
3. Shorten the large straw (axle housing) so it only extends $\frac{1}{2}$ to 1 inch beyond each side of the body of the car. (**NOTE:** The axle housing should not be attached to the car body yet.)
4. Slide the open end of the axle through the straw.
5. Attach the second wheel to the axle.
6. Connect a second axle housing, the other axle, and wheels in the same way.

TIGHTENING THE WHEEL

Sometimes the wheel fits perfectly. Sometimes it just needs to be twisted into place so that it is perfectly perpendicular to the axle and will roll freely on the ground.

Perpendicular (Correct)	Off Center (Not Correct)

TIPS FOR TIGHTENING THE WHEEL

1. Use crossed paper clips to keep the wheel firmly in place and upright. Place one small paper clip over the straw next to the wheel and tape it onto the wheel.
2. Place a second small paper clip over the straw next to the wheel—at right angles to the first paper clip. Tape it to the wheel.
3. You can tape the paper clips on the inside of the wheel or the outside—or on both sides if you want a more secure wheel.
4. You can slit the end of the straw and tape the slit ends to the outside of the wheel to make the wheel more sturdy and straight.
5. Rubber bands can also be used to keep the wheels upright. Wrap the rubber band several times in a tight loop next to each side of a wheel.

MAKING A RACER

ASSEMBLING THE RACER—WHEEL ARRANGEMENTS

Decide where you want the wheels to be located on your racer. Suggestions:

- Don't attach the wheels too close to each other or they will rub against each other and interfere with the speed of the racer.

- You may want to avoid placing the wheels too close to the ends of the vehicle. The middle may drag.

- You may want to use different-sized-wheels on the rear (or front) of your vehicle, or you may want to use same-sized wheels on the front and back.

- Expect to relocate your wheel and axle setup after you have done several trials. You will need to experiment to find the best locations for both speed and distance.

ATTACHING THE WHEEL AND AXLE TO THE BODY

1. You now have two axle units—one for the front and one for the back of your car—with wheels attached firmly to either end of the axle.

2. Make sure all wheels are upright and that both axles spin freely in their axle housing (the larger straw).

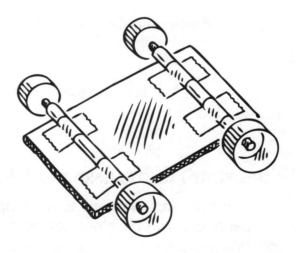

3. Tape the front axle housing to the front of the car and the rear axle housing to the back of the car. Make sure the tape is secure.

4. Test the wheels by whirling them to see if they move swiftly and freely.

MAKING A RACER

JOURNAL ENTRY

1. Describe any problems you had in making your racer. Which activity took the most time, care, and precision? Why?

   _____

   _____

   _____

2. Which part of your racer needs improvement—wheels, body, axle, or some other part?

   _____

   _____

   _____

3. What changes are you going to make to improve the vehicle? _____

   _____

   _____

   _____

4. What do you want to do to make your car faster, more attractive, or stronger?

   _____

   _____

   _____

5. How are you intending to test your car? _____

   _____

   _____

6. What is your next step? _____

   _____

   _____

DESIGN PROCESS REVIEW—MAKING A RACER

Share your journal entries and racers with your classmates during a discussion led by your teacher.

DESIGNING YOUR RACER

You will continue using the same materials as in the previous activity. There are also a few other materials listed for adding weight on the next page. You will be designing your racer to become more efficient and streamlined. If you started with a rectangular box, you can try cutting away some of the box. Make sure that you don't weaken the frame of your racer by cutting away too much or cutting into the strength of the box at the corners or along the ridges. Cars made with Styrofoam™ trays can also be decorated and sculpted by cutting away some of the Styrofoam™.

DECORATING RACERS

You can use glue and tape to add ornamental features to the racer. These could include doors, windows made of clear plastic, bumpers, headlights, and other features.

AERODYNAMIC STYLING

Cars that allow the wind to slide smoothly over and around them go faster because there is less resistance created by air. Try the following techniques to reduce air resistance.

1. Add a triangular wedge to the front of your vehicle so that molecules of air will slide back and away.

2. Carve or sculpt some smooth, curving Styrofoam™ pieces to glue to the front of the racer so that air goes over and around the car body.

3. You may want to cover your vehicle with a completely curved tray or bowl to achieve an aerodynamic effect. You could cut a Styrofoam™ tray or bowl in two and fit the pieces over the entire car to make a low, sleek, sloping vehicle. You can also try using manila folder pieces or tag board to create this streamlined, sports-car effect.

BALANCING DESIGN WITH STRENGTH

- You can use craft sticks or some stiff cardboard to strengthen the sides or base of your racer.
- You may want to add a spoiler to the rear of your racer like some sports cars have. Part of a craft stick, Styrofoam pieces, or tagboard can all be used to make a spoiler.

DESIGNING YOUR RACER

MOMENTUM MATTERS

Your racer will go faster or slower based on several considerations:

1. *the shape and design of the body*

2. *the amount of friction between the axle and the axle housing*

3. *the friction between the wheels and the ramp*

4. *the weight of the vehicle*

A clunky, heavy racer may go too slowly. A really light racer may not have enough weight to create momentum. You will have to balance these factors as you do trials.

ADJUSTING WEIGHT

You can help adjust the momentum of your racer by adding weight to just the right location. Too much weight will slow down your vehicle. Too little weight or weights in the wrong place will also slow down your car. You need to experiment with the proper amount of weight for your car and its best placement.

Weights you can use include:

- canisters of sand
- coins
- containers of water
- marbles

- modeling clay
- nuts and bolts
- pebbles

- pieces of wood
- play dough
- small batteries

ADJUSTING WEIGHTS AND LOCATIONS

1. Try loading one or two AA or AAA batteries along the rear axle, in the center of the body, or try attaching them to the front or rear end of the racer.

2. You may also add one or several small batteries or marbles in the body of the racer.

3. Modeling clay or play dough can be spread along the base of the racer.

4. Lumps of clay with marbles or pennies can be placed in a line along the nose of the racer or at the rear of the car.

5. One or two film canisters—or small cups with caps or masking tape covers—can be filled with sand, water, or small stones in the front, rear, or along the sides of the racer.

NAME

DESIGNING YOUR RACER

TRYOUTS

You can't really improve your racer unless you try it out after each time you add a feature or distribute the weight in a different manner. It is especially important to time your racer with a stopwatch or with a comparison car.

As a ramp, you can use a simple board or a piece of plywood about 2 feet wide and 4 feet long. Skateboard ramps are excellent, too. A folding table with the legs folded in at one end works well, also. Any inclined area with a wide flat surface will work. Take turns with other teams testing your racers.

TIME TRIALS

1. Measure the length of the ramp you are using. Tape the metersticks (or yardsticks) in place down the center of the ramp, if possible.
2. Set two cars in place at the rear of the ramp with the rear wheels just on the ramp.
3. Use a watch or stopwatch to time the trial.
4. Record the time for each trial on this sheet.
5. Do several trials.

Name of Your Racer: _____

TRIAL	LENGTH	TIME
1st		
2nd		
3rd		
4th		
5th		
6th		
7th		

NAME ____________________

Designing Your Racer

Time Trials—Long Course

Directions:

1. Start your long course with the ramp you've been using.
2. Set the ramp on a floor in a classroom, the multi-purpose room, in the cafeteria or gym, or on a walkway or sidewalk where the vehicles can run freely and will stay on course.
3. You may want to use guide rails made of cardboard, short lawn fencing, or some other materials to keep the racers contained along one route.
4. If you have a wide and clear floor area, such as a cafeteria or gym floor, you can simply measure the distance from the top of the ramp to the place where the racer stops. This will allow you to determine the length for each trial.
5. Record the time and distance (length) for each trial on the new record sheet.
6. Do several trials.

Time Trials

Name of Your Racer: ____________________

TRIAL	LENGTH	TIME
1st		
2nd		
3rd		
4th		
5th		
6th		
7th		

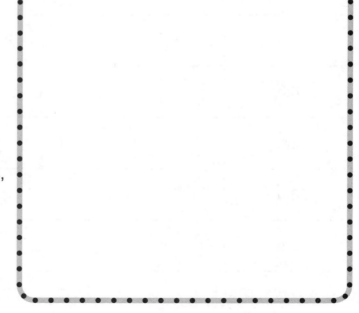
N A M E

DESIGNING YOUR RACER

IMPROVING YOUR RACER

Here are some general principles for improving the speed of your racer:

1. It is often preferable to have the weight in the rear of the vehicle or balanced in the center. You will have to try different arrangements to determine what is best for your racer.

2. The faster your wheel and axle turn, the faster your vehicle will go down the ramp. Check your wheel and axle for obstructions. Smooth out any bumpy spots on the wheel.

3. If your car always turns to one side instead of going straight down the ramp, readjust the wheel and axle or a wheel's location on the axle.

4. If the car seems "sticky" or generally slow as it goes down the ramp, reduce friction on the wheels by smoothing them. A small piece of fine-grade sandpaper will often work for this purpose.

5. Increase traction on the surface of the wheels if they seem to slip when going down the ramp. A thin strip of masking tape can function as a good tire tread.

EXPERIMENTS AND MODIFICATIONS

Try these different designs and modifications to increase the speed of your vehicle.

1. Move the wheel and axle units closer to each other or farther apart to see if you can increase the speed of the vehicle.

2. Try using larger wheels in front or especially on the rear.

3. Try using different wheel materials.

4. Raise or lower the center of gravity for your vehicle. This will probably require different wheel arrangements.

5. Change the contours of your racer by designing a different front end or an entirely different body design.

6. Think outside the box. Make an entirely different car body—possibly using tubes, a can, a small egg carton or egg carton lid, an empty (or partially filled) water bottle, a round plastic bowl, or some other object.

7. Sketch your modified racer in the box.

DESIGNING YOUR RACER

JOURNAL ENTRY

1. Which wheel arrangement worked best for you? Were the front and rear wheels the same size and made the same way, or were they different? Were they close to the ends of the car, near the center, or arranged some other way?

_____

_____

_____

2. What was your biggest problem in making your car work well as a racer? How did you solve the problem?

_____

_____

_____

3. What would you do differently if you were starting over on a new car? What materials would you use this time for the body of the car? What would you use for wheels?

_____

_____

_____

4. Which racer design in your classroom seemed to be most effective and fastest? Why was it so fast? What special features did the car have? What could you learn from it?

_____

_____

_____

5. What is the most important thing you learned about making a race car when you did this activity?

_____

_____

_____

DESIGN PROCESS REVIEW—DESIGNING YOUR RACER

Share your journal entries and racers with your classmates during a discussion led by your teacher.

RACING THE CARS

One-on-one car races are very good for determining the relative speed and distance each car can achieve compared to other cars created by your classmates.

Decide on the kind of ramp you are going to use. Try to find one with good, stable elevation on one end and a long, straight slope. These features will help all of the vehicles go faster. Folding tables work very well for this activity.

You can determine the winners in three ways:

1. The first car to touch the bottom of the ramp
2. The first car to have have all four wheels on the floor
3. The first car to reach a finish line marked on the floor—perhaps a yard or two past the ramp

Participants need to decide beforehand which standard will apply.

Use a long, thin piece of wood (such as a yardstick) to divide the ramp. One racer will be positioned on each side of the barrier. Each racer should start with the rear wheels at the very top edge of the ramp.

1. Choose a judge and someone to start the race. That person should say: **Ready, Set, Go.**
2. Release your car on "**Go.**" **You may not push your car.** You must just let it go and allow momentum to carry the car down the ramp.

MULTIPLE RACERS

Allowing several cars to compete with each other at the same time requires a wide ramp or driveway. Since it is difficult to find barriers for several lanes, you may want to use sidewalk chalk to outline lanes or starting positions. If you have multiple available, thin pieces of wood, metersticks, or yardsticks work best for dividing lanes.

USING TIMERS

Another way to race is to use a single ramp and time the speed of each racer from the moment of release to the time it crosses the finish line. You would need either a stopwatch or a watch that indicates both minutes and seconds.

MEASURING DISTANCE

You can also use a single ramp and determine the winner on the basis of how far each vehicle traveled. Use chalk or masking tape to mark where each car stops, then measure the distance.

RACING THE CARS

After racing your car, you may wish to make more adjustments to make it even faster. Below are some suggestions. Try at least one of them.

THREE WHEELERS

Some derby cars work very well using three instead of four wheels. It is important to make sure the middle wheel is carefully centered. Leave plenty of space for the wheel to move freely if it is inside the frame. You may want to try a larger or smaller wheel for the third wheel.

FIVE WHEELERS

Sometimes a fifth wheel centered at the front or rear of the vehicle adds speed or stability to your racer.

SIX WHEELERS AND EIGHT WHEELERS

You may want to add a double set of wheels to the rear of your vehicle to give it a truck-like look.

You can use four wheels lined up on each side for an eight-wheeler design or two sets of double wheels for a tough truck design.

AIR-POWERED VEHICLES

You can mount a sail on your vehicle and allow the wind to push your racer. Try both square sails and triangular shapes. You can use a hair dryer or small electric fan to make your own wind if it is not windy outside. (You'll need an electrical outlet and extension cord.)

BALLOON-POWERED CARS

Blow up a balloon. Point the top of the balloon toward the front of the vehicle. Use a tight clothespin to keep the balloon inflated. Use two pieces of tape to attach the balloon to the car. Release the clothespin when you are ready. Try balloons of different shapes.

Ⓝ Ⓐ Ⓜ Ⓔ _____

RACING THE CARS

JOURNAL ENTRY

1. Which of the designs and suggestions in this activity worked best for you? Why?

   _____

   _____

   _____

   _____

2. Which design that you saw or worked with was the most interesting? Why?

   _____

   _____

   _____

   _____

3. What is the most important force you had to overcome to make your car go faster? Was it weight, gravity, the friction between wheels and axles, the wind resistance because of the car body shape you chose, or another force? How did you overcome this force?

   _____

   _____

   _____

   _____

4. What would you do differently if you did this project again?

   _____

   _____

   _____

   _____

DESIGN PROCESS REVIEW—RACING THE CARS

Share your journal entries and racers with your classmates during a discussion led by your teacher.

MOTORIZED RACERS

CHALLENGE ACTIVITY—MOTORIZE YOUR RACER

You will work in teams of two to create your own motorized cars based on what you've learned in the previous activities. You may choose to build longer, stronger, bigger, or smaller versions of the types you have already made. The suggested lessons are designed to help you get started if you don't have a specific idea in mind. Use the Design Process Worksheet on page 5 to help guide your work.

TEAM MATERIALS
- 1.5-volt motors with 2 wire leads
- batteries and battery holders or rubber bands
- construction materials and tools from earlier lessons (rulers, scissors, etc.)
- index cards
- paper clips
- poster board or corrugated cardboard
- racers and other vehicles made in earlier lessons

SUGGESTED ACTIVITY # 1
PROPELLER-DRIVEN CARS

Using a motor to power your vehicle requires you to be very careful and meticulous in your work. Follow the instructions below and experiment with different materials until yours is successful.

GETTING STARTED—PREPARING THE CAR

1. Use a large, flat table to build and try out your vehicle.
2. Create a light frame for the car by using a piece of poster board or corrugated cardboard about 6 inches long and 3 inches wide.
3. Use one new battery to power the motor. The batteries must be small and lightweight. Common AA and AAA batteries will be strong enough and light enough, but they are harder to hook up. They also wear out more quickly than C-cell or D-cell batteries. C batteries are heavier but easier to hook to the motor. 9-volt batteries are also a good option.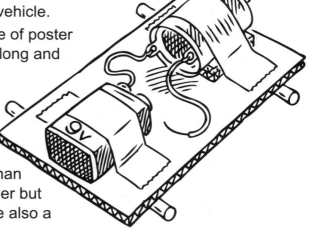
4. Tape a small box or plastic cup to the floor of the roller car to hold the battery and motor.
5. Point the shaft of the motor up.
6. Slit the back of the small box or plastic cup and slip the wires through the slit in the box.
7. Tape over the slit so the motor is firmly held in the box or cup.

MOTORIZED RACERS

CHALLENGE ACTIVITY—MOTORIZE YOUR RACER
COMPLETING THE PROPELLER

1. Tape the wires to the floor of the car, near the box or cup that is holding the motor.

2. Use masking tape or electrical tape to mount the motor securely in the box or cup. **Reminder: The shaft of the motor is pointing out of the end of the open cup or box.**

3. Make a propeller from an index card. Cut an index card into a 2- or 3-inch square. Make four slits and fold each piece into a fan-shaped propeller. Tape the propeller to the shaft of the motor. The propeller should move freely of the car and the cup or box in which the motor is housed.

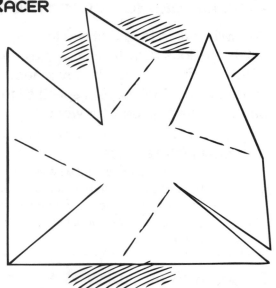

ATTACHING THE BATTERY

1. Place either one or two new or nearly new AA or AAA batteries in an oversized slit straw or tube that can hold the batteries in place.

2. If using two batteries, make sure they are connected with the positive (+) terminal of one battery firmly touching the negative (−) terminal of the other battery. C or D batteries and 9-volt batteries may also be used.

3. Attach one wire from the motor to one terminal of the first battery in the tube. Use electrical or masking tape to keep the wire firmly in place.

PROPELLER-DRIVEN RACERS

1. When you are ready to propel the vehicle, attach the other wire to the other battery terminal by using electrical or masking tape. The fan should rotate rapidly, and the car should move forward.

   NOTE: This model may take patience and several modifications.

2. If the car doesn't move, try these modifications:

   a. Make the car as light as possible by using lighter materials or removing unnecessary weight.

   b. Make the fan either larger or smaller to get more air or greater speed as the fan moves.

   c. Use light, smooth wheels (such as water bottle caps).

   If you want to reverse the direction of the propeller, switch the wires to the opposite terminals of the battery.

   d. Experiment until your propeller-driven car works.

MOTORIZED RACERS

CHALLENGE ACTIVITY—MOTORIZE YOUR RACER
SUGGESTED ACTIVITY #2—SHAFT-DRIVEN MOTOR CARS

1. The motor and battery assembly are the same ones you used for the propeller-driven car. Remove the propeller and turn the motor to the side so that the shaft points to one side of the car.
2. Remove the large straw that holds the rear axle (the rear axle housing). You will need to remove one of the wheels first.
3. Tape two 1-inch-long large-diameter straws—one on each side of the bottom of the car— to hold the wheel and axle. Make sure the wheel and axle rotate smoothly inside the two large diameter straws. Do not connect the wheel yet.
4. Carefully cut a small square or circle in the racer box or base just above the center of the rear axle. The opening could be just about a 2 cm square.

CONNECTING THE MOTOR TO THE SHAFT

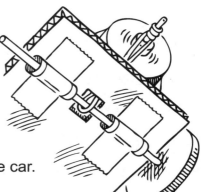

1. Place a rubber band loosely around the rear axle in the middle of the rear of the car.
2. Pull the rubber band through the hole you made in the base of the car.
3. Slip the rubber band over the shaft of the motor. Make sure the rubber band is tight or firm connecting the rear axle to the motor shaft. It should not be rubbing against the bottom of the car.
4. Reattach the wheel you removed and connect the motor.

NOTE: You may need to change rubber bands and make several adjustments until the motor drives the shaft by pulling the rubber band.

MAKING ADJUSTMENTS

1. If the motor doesn't stay connected to the shaft, use a shorter, smaller, or lighter rubber band.
2. If the shaft of the motor is too short to keep the rubber band from coming off, you can extend the shaft by taping a very thin plastic stirrer or straw to it making it longer and less likely to come off. You can slit and bend the straw to make a cap for the shaft.
3. Put a small strip of masking tape around the motor shaft to make it slightly thicker and to hold the stirrer.
4. Fit the stirrer over the shaft. The tape will help it stick securely.
5. Reattach the rubber band to the shaft, which is now longer.
6. Try looping the rubber band in a figure-eight loop to keep it on the shaft.
7. Continue making careful adjustments until the car moves along the table, floor, or ramp.
8. Test your racer, and then race it against other teams.

MOTORIZED RACERS

CHALLENGE ACTIVITY—JOURNAL ENTRY

Use a computer, tablet, or other device to answer each paragraph subject below. Be sure to use paragraph format and complete sentences.

PARAGRAPH 1

What was the hardest part of this activity? Explain in detail.

PARAGRAPH 2

What project did you do to motorize your car? What problems did you encounter? Did your project work?

PARAGRAPH 3

What was the hardest part of the project? Why? How did you overcome the difficulty? Why were teams important?

PARAGRAPH 4

What would you do to improve your motorized car? What other materials would have helped?

PARAGRAPH 5

What was the most successful project you saw in the classroom? Why do you think it worked so well?

PARAGRAPH 6

Respond to these questions by referring back to the activities you completed in this unit.

1. *How can you make a model derby car by using common objects?*
2. *How can you get the derby car to accelerate and travel the fastest from a ramp?*
3. *How can you get the car to travel the farthest distance using its own momentum?*
4. *What is the best size and location for the wheels on the derby car?*
5. *How can you reduce friction and maximize momentum in your derby car?*
6. *What is the relationship between the size of the car and its velocity?*

DESIGN PROCESS REVIEW—MOTORIZED RACERS

Share your racers, describe your efforts, and demonstrate your car in the class discussion/presentations your teacher leads to culminate this unit.

Common Core State Standards

Each lesson meets one or more of the following Common Core State Standards © Copyright 2010. National Governors Association Center for Best Practices and Council of Chief State School Officers. All rights reserved. For more information about the Common Core State Standards, go to *http://www.corestandards.org/* or *http://www.teachercreated.com/standards*.

ELA Reading Science & Technical Subjects Standards	Pages
Key Ideas and Details	
ELA.RST.6.3 Follow precisely a multistep procedure when carrying out experiments, taking measurements, or performing technical tasks.	21–24, 25–30, 31–35, 36–38, 43–47, 48–52, 53–55, 56–57, 62–64, 65–68, 69–71, 72–74, 79–83, 84–87, 88–92, 93–95, 100–103, 104–106, 107–110, 111–115,116–117, 122–125, 126–128, 129–131, 132–135, 140–145, 146–151, 152–154, 155–157
Craft and Structure	
ELA.RST.6.4 Determine the meaning of symbols, key terms, and other domain-specific words and phrases as they are used in a specific scientific or technical context relevant to grades 6–8 texts and topics.	19, 20, 41, 42, 60, 61, 77, 78, 98, 99, 120, 121, 138, 139
Integration of Knowledge and Ideas	
ELA.RST.6.7 Integrate quantitative or technical information expressed in words in a text with a version of that information expressed visually (e.g., in a flowchart, diagram, model, graph, or table).	21–23, 25–29, 31–34, 36–38, 43–46, 48–51, 53–54, 56–57, 62–63, 65–67, 69–70, 72–74, 79–82, 84–86, 88–91, 93–95, 100–102, 104–105, 107–109, 111–114, 116–117, 122–124, 126–127, 129–130, 132–135, 140–144, 146–150, 152–153, 155–157
ELA.RST.6.8 Distinguish among facts, reasoned judgment based on research findings, and speculation in a text.	24, 30, 35, 47, 52, 55, 64, 68, 71, 83, 87, 92, 103, 106, 110, 115, 125, 128, 131, 145, 151, 154
Range of Reading and Level of Text Complexity	
ELA.RST.6.10 By the end of grade 8, read and comprehend science/technical texts in the grades 6–8 text complexity band independently and proficiently.	19, 20, 21–24, 25–30, 31–35, 36–38, 41, 42, 43–47, 48–52, 53–55, 56–57, 60, 61, 62–64, 65–68, 69–71, 72–74, 77, 78, 79–83, 84–87, 88–92, 93–95, 98, 99, 100–103, 104–106, 107–110, 111–115,116–117, 120, 121, 122–125, 126–128, 129–131, 132–135, 138, 139, 140–145, 146–151, 152–154, 155–157

Writing for Science & Technical Subjects Standards	Pages
Text Types and Purposes	
ELA.WHST.6.1 Write arguments focused on discipline-specific content. *(ELA.WHST.6.1B Support claim(s) with logical reasoning and relevant, accurate data and evidence that demonstrate an understanding of the topic or text, using credible sources.)*	24, 30, 35, 36–38, 39, 47, 52, 55, 58, 64, 68, 71, 72–74, 75, 83, 87, 92, 96, 103, 106, 110, 115, 116–117, 118, 125, 128, 131, 136, 145, 151, 154, 158
ELA.WHST.6.2 Write informative/explanatory texts, including the narration of historical events, scientific procedures/ experiments, or technical processes.	24, 30, 35, 36–38, 39, 47, 52, 55, 58, 64, 68, 71, 72–74, 75, 83, 87, 92, 96, 103, 106, 110, 115, 116–117, 118, 125, 128, 131, 136, 145, 151, 154, 158
Production and Distribution of Writing	
ELA.WHST.6.6 Use technology, including the Internet, to produce and publish writing and present the relationships between information and ideas clearly and efficiently.	39, 58, 75, 96, 118, 136, 158

Speaking & Listening Standards	Pages
Comprehension and Collaboration	
ELA.SL.6.1 Engage effectively in a range of collaborative discussions (one-on-one, in groups, and teacher-led) with diverse partners on *grade 6 topics and texts*, and issues, building on others' ideas and expressing their own clearly.	24, 30, 35, 39, 47, 52, 55, 58, 64, 68, 71, 75, 83, 87, 92, 96, 103, 106, 110, 115, 118, 125, 128, 131, 136, 145, 151, 154, 158
Presentation of Knowledge and Ideas	
ELA.SL.6.4 Present claims and findings, sequencing ideas logically and using pertinent descriptions, facts, and details to accentuate main ideas or themes; use appropriate eye contact, adequate volume, and clear pronunciation.	24, 30, 35, 39, 47, 52, 55, 58, 64, 68, 71, 75, 83, 87, 92, 96, 103, 106, 110, 115, 118, 125, 128, 131, 136, 145, 151, 154, 158

Next Generation Science Standards

MS Grade 6. Structure and Properties of Matter	Pages		Pages
Students who demonstrate understanding can:			
MS-PS1-1. Develop models to describe the atomic composition of simple molecules and extended structures.			
Unit 1—Crystal Gardens—Creating Crystals	25–30	Unit 1—Crystal Gardens—Creating Crystal Gardens	31–35
MS-PS1-4. Develop a model that predicts and describes changes in particle motion, temperature, and state of a pure substance when thermal energy is added or removed.			
Unit 1—Crystal Gardens—Exploring the World of Crystals	21–24	Unit 1—Crystal Gardens—Creating Crystals	25–30
		Unit 1—Crystal Gardens—Creating Crystal Gardens	31–35

MS Grade 6. Chemical Reactions	Pages
Students who demonstrate understanding can:	
MS-PS1-2. Analyze and interpret data on the properties of substances before and after the substances interact to determine if a chemical reaction has occurred.	
Unit 5—Kitchen Chemistry	99–118

MS Grade 6. Forces and Interactions	Pages		Pages
Students who demonstrate understanding can:			
MS-PS2-1. Apply Newton's Third Law to design a solution to a problem involving the motion of two colliding objects.			
Unit 7—Derby Cars	139–158		
MS-PS2-2. Plan an investigation to provide evidence that the change in an object's motion depends on the sum of the forces on the object and the mass of the object.			
Unit 2—Go Fly a Kite—Build a Box Kite	48–52	Unit 7—Derby Cars—Designing Your Racer	146–151
Unit 2—Go Fly a Kite—Build a Tetrahedral Kite	53–55	Unit 7—Derby Cars—Racing the Cars	152–154
Unit 2—Go Fly a Kite—Challenge Activity	56–57	Unit 7—Derby Cars—Motorized Racers	155–157
Unit 2—Go Fly a Kite—Challenge Activity (Journal Entry)	58	Unit 7—Derby Cars—Challenge Activity (Journal Entry)	158
MS-PS2-3. Ask questions about data to determine the factors that affect the strength of electric and magnetic forces.			
Unit 3—Static Electricity	61–75		

MS Grade 6. Energy	Pages		Pages
Students who demonstrate understanding can:			
MS-PS3-1. Construct and interpret graphical displays of data to describe the relationships of kinetic energy to the mass of an object and to the speed of an object.			
Unit 7—Derby Cars—Designing Your Racer	146–151	Unit 7—Derby Cars—Challenge Activity (Journal Entry)	158
Unit 7—Derby Cars—Racing the Cars	152–154		

MS Grade 6. Engineering Design	Pages		Pages
Students who demonstrate understanding can:			
MS-ETS1-1. Define the criteria and constraints of a design problem with sufficient precision to ensure a successful solution, taking into account relevant scientific principles and potential impacts on people and the natural environment that may limit possible solutions.			
Unit 2—Go Fly a Kite	42–58	Unit 6—Flying Saucers	121–136
Unit 4—Structures	78–96	Unit 7—Derby Cars	139–158
Unit 5—Kitchen Chemistry—Liquid-Fueled Rockets	111–115		
MS-ETS1-2. Evaluate competing design solutions using a systematic process to determine how well they meet the criteria and constraints of the problem.			
Unit 2—Go Fly a Kite	42–58	Unit 6—Flying Saucers	121–136
Unit 4—Structures	78–96	Unit 7—Derby Cars	139–158
Unit 5—Kitchen Chemistry—Liquid-Fueled Rockets	111–115		
MS-ETS1-3. Analyze data from tests to determine similarities and differences among several design solutions to identify the best characteristics of each that can be combined into a new solution to better meet the criteria for success.			
Unit 2—Go Fly a Kite	42–58	Unit 6—Flying Saucers	121–136
Unit 4—Structures	78–96	Unit 7—Derby Cars	139–158
Unit 5—Kitchen Chemistry—Liquid-Fueled Rockets	111–115		
MS-ETS1-4. Develop a model to generate data for iterative testing and modification of a proposed object, tool, or process such that an optimal design can be achieved.			
Unit 2—Go Fly a Kite	42–58	Unit 6—Flying Saucers	121–136
Unit 4—Structures	78–96	Unit 7—Derby Cars	139–158
Unit 5—Kitchen Chemistry—Liquid-Fueled Rockets	111–115		